THE MISSING FACTOR

What Really is a Normal Christian Life?

Margaret Belanger

authorHOUSE®

AuthorHouse™
1663 Liberty Drive
Bloomington, IN 47403
www.authorhouse.com
Phone: 1-800-839-8640

All names used in the autobiographical, first five chapters, have been changed; including the name of the church they were associated with.

Published by AuthorHouse   01/19/2015

ISBN: 978-1-4969-4806-9 (sc)
ISBN: 978-1-4969-4679-9 (hc)
ISBN: 978-1-4969-4805-2 (e)

Library of Congress Control Number: 2014918486

Scripture quotations marked NKJV are taken from the New King James Version. Copyright © 1982 by "http://www.thomasnelson.com/" Thomas Nelson, Inc. Used by permission. All rights reserved.

CONTENTS

Introduction vii

Preface ix

1   Quest of the Heart 1

2   Beginnings...10

3   Church...14

4   A Means to an End 20

5   Beginning of the End..31

6   What Really Is a Normal Christian Life? 37

7   Propensities and Modus Operandi 41

8   Dogs, Crumbs, and the Law 46

9   New Wine and New Wineskins 51

10   The Good News..55

11   A New Covenant..58

12   He Is Risen...62

13   Salvation: The Eternal Now....................................69

14   Mixing the Covenants..75

15   Trials, Tests, and Tribulations 80

16   What Is Grace?..86

17   Christian Nonbelievers...92

18   The Beautiful Fight of Faith 95

19   Core Stability 101

20   A Trusting Relationship 107

21   Identity: A New Creation......................................115

22   Well Equipped: A True Perspective 123

23   Congruency: Living in God's Reality 131

About The Author...139

INTRODUCTION

"Let's pray for God's protection, as they set out on their trip." The pastor announced.

As we began to pray, there arose within me a sense of doubt, and a feeling of uncertainty. I was a young Christian and I was recalling a recent sermon I had heard on the sovereignty of God. In it he spoke of how God sometimes allows trials and difficulties into our lives to teach, purify, or mature us.

We said the right words in our prayers, but in my heart there raged a nagging question ".Maybe God had something that He wanted to teach them (or us) through some trouble they encounter along the way".

This seems rather bizarre in light of what I know now, but many Christians are (sometimes, without realizing it), caught up in this type of conundrum.

In another church, the pastor was addressing the recent death of a teenage boy who had been diagnosed with cancer a few months earlier. "We don't know why God took this young man, but we cannot understand His ways", the pastor said. Had I known what I understand today, I would have asked him, "Didn't Jesus teach and demonstrate God's will and ways?" Yes, God received this young man into His presence, but does God use disease?

Another time and situation, in a different church, a financial need had arisen and we were praying, "Lord, let it be pleasing to you to look down from heaven upon us". The pastor continued, "We beseech You, Lord, if it be Your will, to see fit to consider our needs and answer our prayers."

It all sounded so good and right and humble (and certainly, out of a desire to honor God) and yet something was amiss. Is this really, how New Covenant Believers are to approach God?

These examples were taken from real situations and took place in accepted mainstream churches. These attitudes and perspectives are not in line with new covenant truth.

What comes to mind when you hear the terms: "salvation", "prayer".. "dying to self".. "faith" or "abundant life"..?

Although familiar terms to every Christian, these words hold very different meaning to different people. Just one of these terms could stir up anything from hair pulling debate to fear and confusion, or inspire joy and anticipation.

What once was a cherished truth, and a personal reality (to Believers), has today, in many ways, become simply a doctrinal creed; a Bible study subject, or a vagary of unattainable aspirations; or in some cases, just a deferred longing for heaven.

Until we understand this new covenant and what Jesus has done for us we will continue to grapple with seeming contradictions and have no confidence in our prayers and our standing in Christ.

Too often we face life's challenges with uncertainty, weak and powerless, having little confidence in who we are and what is ours is Christ. As you read this book you will discover that walking with God, living in victory, and expecting answered prayer is not the exception but can be simply a part of a normal Christian life.

PREFACE

This book is not an autobiography, but I felt it necessary to share a little about my own experiences, in order to offer you some background into my own search and the conclusions I came to and what inspired my passion for New Covenant truth.

My desire is that you will share with me in the wonders of God's faithfulness, love and continued good will for us, sometimes in spite of faulty choices, fears, and misconceptions. So that you also can say that His word is true and His provision through Jesus is sufficient for your particular situation.

In the first five chapters I have touched on some of my own experience. I have included some details of one particular church I was involved in as a young Christian. In the process I have uncovered some key factors, which I believe led us away from the foundations that are ours in Christ.

Through the remainder of the book I will shed light on the fact that these faulty religious perceptions were not so unique to this one church, but they find their way into our thinking and beliefs in many churches today, and stand in contradiction to New Covenant realities.

Step by step you will discover the love and good will of God towards us. My prayer is that you will come to realize more fully (as I have) all that Jesus accomplished for us, and what it means for us in our personal experience.

CHAPTER 1

Quest of the Heart

I have loved you with an everlasting love, therefore
with loving kindness have I drawn thee.
—Jeremiah 31:3

There is something beautiful and profound in the fact that we can
personally, intimately, and actually connect with the Eternal One. It
surpasses scientific calculations; defies intellectual explanation, and it
cannot be contained in religion's delusion. Those who find it cannot
settle for anything less.

I started my journey on a quest (a heart-longing kind of search) for
reality and meaning in life. Although the initial pursuit came out of
an honest and simple desire, the experiences along the way have been
anything but orthodox, or simple. Through it all, God continued with
me, and His faithfulness never failed.

Growing up, I had no concept of what it means to be a Christian.
Neither of my parents, nor any relative, that I know of, had any apparent
inclination towards the things of God. It was something we just didn't
talk about. There was an underlying perception that God existed, but
He remained a foggy, nebulous concept, clothed in confusion and
uncertainty. I never saw a Bible in our home, and (except for a couple
of rare occasions), we never attended a church.

My grandmother, on my mother's side, did take an interest in the
"spiritual". She dabbled in palm reading and fortune telling with cards,
and held to various superstitions. I remember every New Years (shortly

after midnight), she made sure that a man, with dark-colored hair (usually my father or a friend), went out the back door and came in the front. The thought behind this odd practice was that if the first man coming through the front door had light-colored hair, we would have bad luck that year. If he had dark hair, we would be blessed with good luck.

My grandmother became a widow in her late forties. Her husband (my granddad) died from a lung disease, (presumably due to his many years working as a chimney sweep as a young man, in the 1930's. Consequently, she came with us, when we moved to Canada in the spring of 1955.

At that time my mother's view of 'religion' was a mixture of fear and confusion. She never felt that she was good enough to go to church. I know she believed there is a God, but somehow He was far away and unapproachable.

My father, on the other hand, grew up attending an orthodox Catholic church in Zeromskigo, Poland. As a young teenager, during WWII, he became involved in a "youth Resistance Movement" when Germany occupied Poland. As a result, he spent some time in a concentration camp. Afterwards, he suffered from a form of post-traumatic stress (later diagnosed with Paranoid Schizophrenia).

After making our home in Canada, my father announced that he wanted nothing to do with God. Nevertheless, a wall or two of our house was decked with pictures of various saints. (I can only assume it was Dad who put them there, as no one else had any association with anything religious). One portrayed a 'saint' who was said to watch over us as we slept. A similar icon hung on the mirror of the car to "keep us safe on the road". Although, perhaps intellectually, he rejected the God he didn't know, I believe in his tormented soul, he yearned for a God who cared.

I remember attending a Christmas Mass in a Catholic church. I must have been about seven and my brother Rick, was eight. The experience made God seem strange and mysterious, to me, and I left with the impression that our attendance was a means to elicit some kind of "good luck" for the coming year.

As a child, I later had a kind of idealistic view of Christians. I saw them in light of some movie or TV program I had seen, (like *"Father Knows Best"*. They were all, I assumed, upper-middle-class;

happy families, who lived in beautiful homes in the suburbs. I imagined that they lived safe and predictable lives, so unlike my own, at the time. And, of course, they all attended church on Sundays. What they did there, I had no idea.

In spite of all the confusion surrounding my perception as a child, today, in retrospect, I can testify to God's continued working throughout my life.

The fact is, as a child, home was not a safe place; it was often filled with uncertainty and fear.

"They are conspiring against me, and their intention is to destroy me and my family," My father told my mother. "Who are 'they'?" Mum asked him. They were the voices he heard in his head.

He shared these and similar things with my mother. He said that he was afraid that "they" would take away his children, (Rick and me). He was afraid that if we ever saw him again, we wouldn't recognize him (these were the fears he lived with). He slept with a loaded gun beside his bed. Although Rick and I were only about eleven and ten by then, Mum shared these things with us.

There were the occasional times of perceived normality. At Christmas-time, for instance, we'd gather in the living room together, sharing gifts and enjoying special treats we didn't normally eat. In summer, Dad would take us to "the river". I'm not certain where exactly this was, but it was a quiet, secluded, (and safe) place, in the country, by a river just outside of Montreal. Rick, Dad. and I would swim and laugh together. I knew that he enjoyed these times, but still he was distant, and he always seemed preoccupied in his mind.

If you have ever seen the movie, *"Beautiful Mind"* you might have an idea of my dad's inner life. He was very intelligent, spoke several languages, and had begun to attend university before the war started, but none of this helped him. He couldn't keep a job. He was a taxi driver for some time, and then he worked for a moving company.

I can remember, when I was about eight years old, lying in bed, and hearing my parents arguing in the next room. They were shouting and shoving one another, and things were crashing to the floor. Although I was troubled by it all, I lie there talking to God and feeling comforted.

Maybe it was the result of a seed sown by something I had read, or maybe it was the hymns we occasionally sang in school, in those days. One song in particular that I loved to sing, and still remember some of the words: "This is my Father's world; I rest me in the thought of rocks and trees, of skies and seas; His hand the wonders wrought." (I suppose this resonated with me because of my love for nature). another verse tells of how, "He shines in all that's fair: in the rustling grass I hear Him pass; He speaks to me everywhere." It made a significant impression on my heart. I knew that He was there and that He heard me. A kind of intuitive, inner sense drew me to reach out to a God I didn't yet know or understand.

As time went on, Dad's illness grew worse (I don't think there was much understanding, council, or treatment at that time), he became more obsessed with his delusional antagonists. At one point he drove a man down in the street, because he just knew that this man was part of the conspiracy. He spent some time in prison, and underwent some counsel. Shortly thereafter, he and Mum separated, and finally, Mum, Rick, and I, as well our grandmother, moved away.

Twice we moved just outside of Montreal, but Dad always found us. During those times, he would ask me if I wanted to go with him. I was eleven years old, and the situation was difficult. I was afraid of him, but he was my dad. A short time later, he moved back to Poland, and we didn't hear from him again, (until I was an adult).

Shortly after this, Ronny came into our lives. He had become a friend and confidant of Mum's during the tumultuous times with Dad. At the time, she was working at a hospital in Montreal, in the "central supply" (laundry department), and Ronny also worked there.

After the divorce, we all moved to Chateauguay, just off the island of Montreal. Chateauguay was a good place in which to live and grow up. At that time, it was half rural, and the rest was a growing housing development. Rick and I both have some good memories of our time there. We were in our teens, and for the most part, good friends.

It wasn't exactly smooth sailing with Ronny. He had many qualities, but being a father figure was not one of them (at least as far as Rick and I were concerned). Ronny suffered from regular bouts of depression, and he would consequently spend several days in bed; with that, of course, came the loss of jobs, accumulating bills, and raging conflicts between him and Mum.

I suppose I just simply accepted Ronny for who he was (and expected nothing more). When he wasn't depressed, he took an interest in both history and geography, and he loved to travel. When he was feeling good, Mum, Rick, and I (as well as a large German shepherd named Monty) would cram into a small car and head down to the states. I became familiar with nearly all of the eastern United States.

After my sister, Louise, was born, things slowly began to improve. Ronny found a medication that helped to bring equilibrium between his highs and lows, and he was better equipped to keep a job. After that, Ronny, Mum, and Louise went on a few trips overseas. Occasionally they would visit his mother and aunt in Brussels, Belgium. Every year around Christmas, Ronny's mother would send a package containing a few small gifts and some Belgium chocolate, for Louise. Apparently Ronny had neglected to tell his mother that the woman he's married had two other children from a previous marriage.

These experiences didn't do much for my feelings of self-worth, none the less, I did love my little sister, and I enjoyed watching her grow from an infant to a child. Since Rick and I left home when Louise was about seven, I didn't really get to know her until years later, when she was a young adult.

While growing up, Rick and I continued to be close friends, probably due to the fact that we had moved quite often. Although each of us had other friends, we'd frequently end up just hanging out together. Later, there were three of us; Rick, Michael Judson, and me. Michael and Rick became friends in high school. I joined the dynamic threesome after I graduated from the same high school a year later. Sometimes the three of us would go out for a drink or two together, or we'd just sit and chat. Both Michael and Rick had a great sense of humor and they kept me laughing. Although they both dated various girls, and I had boyfriends over the years, Michael, Rick, and I remained good friends.

In my late teens, my life was full of many things, but there was a gnawing emptiness within me. It seemed to me, that the whole world around me was drifting along in a fog of meaningless endeavors. I had a boyfriend, who, at one point, said to me, "You're deep." He wasn't a Christian, (and neither was I). I suppose it was just his way of saying, "What's the matter with you?" "Just relax and enjoy life!" "Forget about the 'meaning' of things.. there isn't any."

I had a part-time job, and I had also begun doing some art work. A friend of Ronny's, who was himself an artist, encouraged me in my create abilities, by giving me some oil paints and a few helpful tips.

In the 1960's and 70's, I also began to take an interest in "folk" music. I gravitated to Bob Dylan, Joan Baez, and many more musicians whose songs spoke of social issues, poverty, injustice, and senseless wars (in which no one wins). The songs seemed to echo my own sense of longing.

Around that time, I became friends with Carol Conner. I met her in a coffee shop in Chateauguay. She was really into the "folk" music scene and the music I liked. She had a boyfriend who played in a band, and she occasionally sang for them. She had a beautiful voice that was equal to (if not better than) the voice of Joan Baez.

The main thing, though, that we had in common was the fact that we were both searching, and in desperate need of Jesus Christ. At the time, we didn't fully realize what or whom we were looking for.

Carol and I spent many hours sitting at her kitchen table, sipping coffee. When the conversation lagged, she'd pour another cup, and on we went. With all the coffee we drank, I'm surprised that we weren't wired and vibrating by the time we finished.

Together, we delved into Eastern religions, (which were in vogue at the time). We attended a Yoga camp, tasted Transcendental Meditation, and swayed to the drones of Ravi Shankar playing his sitar. We tried to get in touch with nature, and in tune with the cosmos, but neither of us found what we were looking for there.

One day, at Carol's place, I reached across to the book-shelf and took out the large, old, tattered, dusty Bible. We had read small parts of the Old Testament together at other times, but it had all seemed rather confusing. She had also shared with me her own experience of attending a Catholic church ears earlier, but it had all seemed strange and mysterious to her, and she hadn't continued there for very long.

This time, though, I held the book, feeling the weight of it in my hands, and I randomly flipped it open to the book of Ecclesiastes, (which speaks of a man's search for meaning). I was taken aback by the fact that some of the very same questions and concerns I had, were, in fact, in the Bible. I didn't pursue the matter any further, at the time. Carol and I simply go talking about other things, and then went on our ways.

It was late March in 1969, and the snow in Montreal had already turned from gray slush to a few wet patches on the street. I was job hunting.

It had been almost two years since I graduated from Howard S. Billings High School, but instead of continuing my education, I had decided to get a job. I was undecided as to what direction to go, and of course, I would need much more money than I had to even begin to pursue any further studies. My French was not as fluent as it needed to be in order to get a job in Quebec. So getting a good-paying job, and one that I'd like was rather challenging.

As I sat for a moment in the park, I was approached by a tall, slim man, (probably in his early twenties), wearing a T-shirt, well-worn jeans, and sandals. His hair was tied back with a multi-colored band. He introduced himself as Arpad and sat down beside me. My thoughts drifted to his rather attractive features, and the fact that I was not going out with anyone at the time.

"Do you know that Jesus loves you?" He asked me. I said something like, "Yes, I think so." But I wasn't entirely sure what that really meant. We didn't talk for long, but as we parted, he handed me an address and invited me to attend a church service, where a visiting ministry would be speaking.

The following day, I did attend, along with Rick, and my friend Carol. There was no church building, as such, but the service was held in a large conference room adjacent to McGill University campus.

As I hesitantly approached the door of the building, I noticed a well-dressed man, probably West Indies/Canadian, (I guessed, by his medium-dark skin color and black hair). He greeted me with a broad smile and said, "Yes, you're in the right place!" Time would tell if that was the case.

The songs they sang were unfamiliar, but the singing carried a sense of genuineness and earnestness. A few people got up and shared briefly. Some spoke of difficult situations they were facing and asked for prayer, and they also shared about how God's Presence comforted them.

It seemed good, and all was well, until a stocky little man (apparently, the visiting ministry) made his way to the platform. He was briefly introduced as Stan Piper, and unhampered by formalities, he began to speak. I sensed an air of arrogance about him, as he proceeded to shout, spit, and cough out a message that alluded to an angry, exacting God, and our call to "sinless perfection". He spoke of "dying to self" as a process of God with the purpose of "purging away our sins." At least, this was the essence of what I was able to decipher from his very lengthy dissertation.

Stan's words weighed heavily on my heart. I recalled my first childhood experience with God. I had come to see Him as "Father" through the years that followed. Now I wondered if He was going to have to purge me to make me sinless. I left there, troubled and confused. It was then that I resolved to more earnestly search out this matter myself.

Rick seemed unfazed by the speaker, but like me, he chose not to return to that church. Later that summer, he and a few friends attended the play, *"Jesus Christ Super Star"*. It had a profound effect on him, and shortly afterward, he gave his heart to the Lord.

Carol told me that she was not interested in attending that "church" again, and she advised me not to do so either.

I was nineteen and I had begun to seek God in the best way I knew. Around this time, I happened to find, tucked away in a box (at my mum's house), a small New Testament, that I had forgotten I had. It had been given to me, years earlier, at a 'Kid's summer program' put on at a Baptist church. I'd probably been around twelve when a friend had invited me to attend. All I remember about it were the missionary stories, the crafts, a Halloween party, and the little book that I'd received.

Now, years later, this tiny, leather-bound book was to hold for me much greater significance.

By this time, I had a full-time job, up St. Laurent Street in Montreal. A Jewish clothing factory. I started out sewing labels onto pants, and later ended up in the office, mostly doing invoices for orders. It wasn't the greatest job, but it was a job. It was there that I met a man I ended up going out with for three and a half years.

He was from Trinidad and introduced me to Calypso music and steel bands. It was great fun. We spent a lot of time at "Man and His World" which was a continuation of Expo '67. There were many sights representing different countries, as well as an array of restaurants offering a variety of international dishes. We had a great relationship and could talk about anything.

I was still living in Chateauguay at the time, so I had a forty-five minute bus ride to and from work in Montreal every day. I decided to take advantage of this time, thinking it was a good opportunity for me to read my little book.

Within the pages, beyond the historic accounts and teachings, I began to encounter a Person, whose words, somehow bypassed my intellect, and awakened my heart to an unconditional love. It had a profound effect on me.

I can't say that I was immediately convicted of my sins, (though they were certainly there), but His love was not limited by religious protocols, or formulas. "You shall seek me and you shall find me," the Lord said, through Jeremiah, "when you shall search for me with all your heart."

As I continued to read, I wasn't aware of the route the bus was taking or the time that had passed. The sense of his Presence was so real to me that it was palpable. It was as if, at that moment, my eyes were opened, and I understood that God was not mysterious, or aloof, and as Jesus promised, His Spirit came to abide in my heart. No longer did I have to be bound by my fears, insecurities, and superstitions. He was "the Vine" (to support, nourish, and enable me to grow and mature), and I was a "branch" joined to Him through faith in Him. I understood that it was an abiding, (ongoing relationship that) had to be internal, (in my heart). In this way, it would have an effect on my thoughts, emotions, and decisions throughout life).

It was raining, and little droplets were gently washing their way down the dirty window of the bus, even as tears flowed down my cheeks, and His love washed away the pain I had held in my heart from childhood.

As the bus finally arrived at the terminus on Dorchester Street, in Montreal on that rainy April morning, I looked around at the people rushing past me, and I felt a love for them beyond my own capacity. This unfamiliar feeling lifted me out of the cloud of self-protection that had followed me, (one where people were something to be avoided at all costs).

It is true that when we first come to the Lord, a great change takes place, but it takes time, (a lifelong journey) to know Him, and to grow and mature. As well, the healing of the heart is a process.

CHAPTER 2

Beginnings

"For we are made partakers of Christ
if we hold the beginning of our confidence stedfast unto the end."
—Hebrews 3:14 (KJV)

The first few years of walking in this newfound reality were nothing less than amazing. Having no preconceived views to complicate my walk with the Lord, faith was simple, real, and practical. I had an inner sense of peace and confidence that I hadn't known before. It felt as though I was walking through life enveloped in His love.

I had a sense of peace and inner confidence that was beyond my previous norm. I even started writing poetry in those days. I had always liked to write and express myself on paper, but this was different. Words now flowed out of my heart with wisdom beyond my own. If something was troubling me, I'd begin writing, and words of comfort and council would flow poetically. (I'm not saying, I was taken over and my hand just began writing; but words and thoughts filled with my newfound faith in God, just flowed out of my heart).

I remember a situation where I was obligated to talk with a coworker who had always intimidated me. Instead of worrying, I said, "I don't have to worry, the Lord is with me!" On the way back to work, I began singing to myself songs with words like: "The Lord is my light and my salvation; whom shall I fear?" and "He strength of my life; of whom shall I be afraid?" By the time I arrived back at work, I felt empowered.

As my co-worker and I talked, we were able to work through the problems and find a solution.

Prayer, for me, was almost, one might say, childlike in its simplicity. I assumed every believer knew God in this way. In prayer, I came to Him expecting Him to be there, and I was never disappointed. Whether I was kneeling beside my bed, sitting at the kitchen table, or walking down the street, I felt His presence with me. Often-times I was aware of a deep, inner kind of longing, urging me to spend time in His presence, in prayer. (I can't say that I always responded, but when I did, He was there.

I confided in Him, as one would, with a close friend. When He seemed far away, I always recognized eventually, the fact that it was my own heart that was distracted. (Through challenging circumstances over the years, I have always found Him to be my confidant and help).

During those early years, I also experienced several physical healings. At one point, I was suffering from a severe case of eczema on the insides of my thighs. It was extremely itchy and irritating, and scratching only made it worse, causing the rash to spread. Finally, in desperation, I decided to see a doctor about it. On the way to his office, I experienced an inner conviction, and I thought, "I don't need to do this; I am a child of God, now." I went anyway, since I had already made an appointment.

The doctor prescribed some cream that was supposed to alleviate the symptoms. When I got home and was holding the tube of cream in my hand, I said to myself, "I don't need this." I threw the tube of cream in the garbage, and within a short time, I was healed. The fact is, I didn't even think about it until three days later. Then I noticed that it wasn't bothering me anymore, and I realized that the rash was completely gone.

Many such experiences were simply a part of my brother Rick's and my life, at that time. There was a sense of dignity and dominion. We knew that all things were possible.

One day while Rick was at work, (in his cabinet shop), it was particularly busy, and other carpenters were busily working on various projects. Through the din of table saws and drills, Rick began to sing praises to God, and suddenly he was worshipping in another language, the kind spoken of in Acts 2:4, and 1 Corinthians 12:10). He told me later that this new-found sense of God's presence was with him throughout the day.

When Rick was twenty and I was nineteen we decided that it was time to move out of our family home. Rick had never really gotten along with Ronny, and I felt it was time for me to go also. So, once again, the three of us, Rick, Michael, and myself, packed up and headed for Montreal. We found a three bedroom apartment in the Westmount district of Montreal. This arrangement provided us with the convenience of being closer to work for both Rick and I; as well as sharing the cost of rent.

I was still working at the clothing factory, up St. Laurent Street, on the east side of Montreal. It was still a bit of a distance, as I had to take the Metro (subway) part-way and then a city bus the rest of the way, but it was still faster and more convenient than the forty-five minute bus commute from Chateauguay.

Rick continued working as a cabinet-maker, and Michael worked in an accounting office with a view to becoming an accountant.

We all shared similar interests and liked some of the same kinds of music; such as Simon and Garfunkel, The 5th Dimension, and Gordon Lightfoot, and other popular music of the seventies. We even attended concerts together, at "Place des Arts". We were good friends, and we shared some stimulating conversations, but regrettably, at the time, Michael had no interest in God.

For Rick and me, these were exciting times. Sometimes on the weekends, Rick and I would sit and talk about what God had been speaking in our hearts that week. It truly was an amazing time.

It wasn't long, though, before we began to feel a need to connect with other believers. We found a Bible study group, in Montreal just below Sherbrook Street. It was put on by "Youth for Christ" ministries, and we began attending in the evenings right after work. We didn't always have time to stop for supper, it didn't matter to us; we were so excited about what we were learning.

The Bible study took place in a small hall near McGill University. Most of those attending were students at the university. We had some lively discussions with pastor Ron Wallace, who led the studies. Apart from his very sanguine personality, which bordered on loud and overpowering, I witnessed his genuine love for the Lord, and was often inspired by his faith and his insight into the Word of God.

I thoroughly enjoyed the studies and ravenously devoured every word. During that time, I gained some vital foundations to my understanding of the scriptures, and a love for studying that has continued to this day.

Understanding the difference between the two testaments, the old and the new, was a revelation to me. This made it easier for me to understand the way God related to His people both under the old covenant and the new. It helped me to see the underlying theme of God's love and purpose for mankind unfolding through the testaments and bringing salvation through Jesus. Most of all, though, Pastor Ron taught us about our new Life in Christ.

It was with Ron that several of us were baptized in a swimming pool in Montreal. And late in that same year, Ron and a few other ministries prayed with me to receive the baptism of the Holy Spirit.

I remember one particular study that stuck with me for many years afterward. It was when Pastor Ron shared the fact that Christ lives in us by His Spirit. He explained that, when we read or hear God's Word, it isn't just information. We must take it into our hearts and lives. As an illustration, Ron picked up the glass of water beside him and drank from it. This, to me was a graphic picture of how God's Word can become part of us and affect our lives. As I considered this, I imagined myself taking His Word into my heart where it transformed my thoughts and feelings, permeating every part of me and producing strength where there as weakness and equipping me as His disciple.

Within a short time, Rick and I began attending the church that Ron Wallace was a part of, as did some of the young people who had come to the Lord through "Youth for Christ". The church was located on a side street near McGill, fittingly called University Street. Ironically this was the same church that Rick, Carol, and I had first attended one evening almost a year earlier when we heard Stan Piper preach. Within the past year, much had changed in my life (and in Rick's) and now, of course, the visiting minister was long gone, and with him my reservations.

CHAPTER 3

Church

"Onward and upward into greater and higher things."
Winston Churchill

The church on University Street was birthed out of a people's desire for genuine New Testament Christianity.

We were a conglomeration of nationalities and church affiliations. Montreal in the sixties and seventies was a multicultural city, so we consisted of Chinese, Italians, Jamaicans, Sri Lankans, as well as French, Scottish, and English, and a few born-and-bred Canadians.

They were sincere and genuine people with a heart after God. Many had come out of Assemblies of God, Pentecostal churches, some were from other denominations, and a few, like myself, were new believers.

There was also a wide variety of ages, from young families to a few elderly people, and everything in between. Such diversity made for a colorful, healthy, and challenging environment.

The common denominator, from the start, was an honest desire for real, authentic, and practical New Testament Christianity.

Most of the people there had left their churches because hey were dissatisfied with what they felt were empty forms and structures. They sought the "life" and "reality" they seemed to have lost after many years of walking with the Lord. Some said that they had come to the point where the traditions and programs, as good as they may have been, now seemed empty, having little to do with their lives as believers. In essence, the common question was, "Is this all the Christian life is about?"

In the early days, we felt as though we were free and unencumbered with empty religious forms and structures. We wanted to be "led by the Spirit, like the early church of the New Testament", we thought. Granted, there may have been some unorthodox ideas and practices that have evolved in various groups, from such out-of-the-box thinking, but I have no doubt that the early believers, or Paul himself, would certainly think what we consider "normal" church strange, if they attended it today.

At the beginning of church services, usually during the praise service before the pastor (in this case, *pastors*) preached, anyone could get up and share, and many did. It was a normal part of the service. The time involved was flexible. Sometimes, if several people shared, it could go on for half an hour or more. Some people gave thanks to God and testified of an answer to prayer. Occasionally, individuals would share poems or songs they had been inspired to write. Many just shared what God had been speaking to their hearts or doing in their lives. This candid sharing really drew us together.

The message was usually very pertinent and applicable. It always amazed me how the songs, scriptures, and testimonies shared, more often than not, seemed connected by a common theme, in spite of the fact (or perhaps *because* of the fact) that nothing was planned or prepared beforehand except for the message preached.

There was genuine caring for one another in those days. There were only about sixty of us at the time. Without any programs or schedules, per se, we would rally to the cause whenever a need arose, put on our work gloves, so to speak, and simply help out in whatever ways we could. One time, a young couple moved into an old house, and the hard-wood floors needed redoing. After work one evening, several of us drove to their house (just outside the city), and we spent the evening stripping, sanding, and refinishing the floor. We worked until 1:00 or 2:00 a.m. stopping only to order pizza for a late supper around 7:00 or 8:00. It was great to have the opportunity to put our faith into practice.

As new believers, a few of us got in the habit of sometimes greeting each other with the question, "How are you doing spiritually?" We had a connection with one another that went beyond the shallow surface that some circles today call "*fellowship*". Perhaps we were a bit idealistic, but we knew in our hearts what our lives as believers could be. It wasn't something we just talked about in church, We wanted to live it.

As time went on, there was talk of "community." The messages preached began to allude to the early church in Acts, where believers had all things in common. We started by having meals together after church on Sundays, giving more opportunity for fellowship with one another. Later, there was talk of renting two large apartments in different districts of Montreal, with the idea that we would live together and support and build up one another in the faith. These households would be a place where we could grow and mature in the Lord.

Shortly thereafter, we corporately rented two apartments. They came to be called "body houses," of all things, referring, of course, to the 'body of believers' but it was a term that could send one's imagination running wild. This arrangement lasted a few months. After that, we eventually rented a huge, old mansion at the end of Redpath Crescent, which was located at the foot of Mount Royal (a small mountain in the center of Montreal), where most of the church members moved in together.

It was an immense building, that had previously been owned by stockbrokers. As we entered the front door, we were greeted by a large foyer, a fireplace with an imposing oak mantel, and hardwood floors and walls. It was quite impressive. On one side was a huge oak staircase, and on the other side a door leading to the dining room, kitchen, and butler's pantry. The house also had a large conference room, which we used for services, complete with carvings of a bull and a bear over a fireplace. Although it was old, it was an impressive three-story building. Each bedroom included en suite bathroom and had a fireplace. every couple or family had a room to themselves, while single men occupied a dorm in the basement, and the single "girls" (as we were called) occupied two large dorms on the second and third floors.

At first, it was a bit of an adventure for those of us who were in our early twenties. Most of us were attending university or college or were working, and we were out of the household for much of the time.

In the 'girls' dorm, it appeared that those who were naturally social bloomed, while those who were not so inclined didn't. Inevitably, personality conflicts were a common occurrence, but at the same time, some lasting relationships were formed.

I was always thankful for my friend Dayna, whose hilarious sense of humor, coupled with her love for the Lord, kept me both laughing and encouraged in the Lord. I met Dayna at one of the early services at the church on University Street. She had grown up in the Westmount district of Montreal and had lived in the state of New York for some time as a teenager. (I believe her stepdad was American.) We were quite different in personalities, but as time went on, we became good friends. We spent hours talking about our personal experiences with the Lord. We were on the same page, I believe, spiritually. Little by little, we both later recognized some of the erroneous thinking of the church.

As the weeks turned into months, household life merged with the myriad of day-to-day life experiences, and our relationships grew into a cross between a loving bond and phlegmatic tolerance. I think the idea was that, if given the right environment, Christian love would emerge, and righteous living would eventually evolve (similar to the theory of evolution).

There was, however, a growing, underlying issue that many of us had not noticed at the beginning. I had heard of other small groups who were meeting together, but I didn't fully make the connection or grasp the implications until we began attending "conventions."

After just a few months of living in the "body house," the conventions became part of our biannual tradition. Twice a year, in the fall and at Christmas, we would cross the country in a caravan of Volkswagen vans. In October we attended the convention in Canton, Ohio; and then in December, we went to Miami, Florida. As time went on, this tradition came to include two or three other conventions.

At this time, the church began to call itself "the fellowship."

At the conventions, we once again encountered Stan Piper, this time with several associates who called themselves "apostles" or "father ministers." Before this, we had occasionally heard tapes by Piper and other ministers.

It was here that I began to see a dangerous trend. I saw men and women, especially those in leadership who called themselves "elders," trying to set up a formalized system, which soon evolved into a hierarchy of leadership. It was an attempt to produce in a people something that only God could bring about. Additionally, I witnessed the tendency of people to put a man into a position that God never intended—at the cost of personal responsibility.

Many people idolized "Brother Stan," as he came to be called—and other ministers—assuming they had attained to some great anointing. Followers hung on Stan Piper's every word, going from convention to convention, waiting for the "next line": the message that would take them to the next level of spirituality and on to "perfection."

We were attending another Canton convention, and we had already heard four or five "father ministers" share their messages. Three of them had spoken between 9:00 a.m. and 12:00 noon, and then two others had preached between 1:00 and 4:00 p.m. We were already feeling rather weary (at least I and a few others I knew were), and we were anticipating another especially long message from Brother Piper.

Slowly he rose and made his way to the pulpit. "Turn to Colossians 2:6," he said, and he quickly recited the verse. Then he went on to say, "Most of you will not be able to understand this message until you are ready to enter into 'sonship,' for those who are still at a lesser level in Christian growth cannot understand the deeper things. The books of Ephesians and Colossians are God's sonship books in the New Testament, and it is hard for spiritual teenagers to understand them."

From there he went into a two-hour explanation of various "levels of spirituality" through which we must grow before we can "enter the realm of sons of God." His four levels were: "servantship, discipleship, friendship, and sonship" (as if these terms described degrees of maturity instead of simply aspects of our relationship with God). Ridiculous as it may sound, many people saw Brother Piper as an apostle of the "deeper" truth.

I thought to myself, *Either I'm too immature to understand, or he's complicating something very simple*—something he often tended to do. Colossians 2:6 (KJV) says, "As ye have therefore received Christ Jesus the Lord, so walk ye in him." I thought the so-called "sonship books" simply illustrated aspects of our relationship with God—aspects that we all can experience now."

Many of the other ministers' messages seemed plausible at the time, so I wasn't ready yet to throw out the whole thing.

At that point, I and many others had a lot to learn, and it would take some time and experiences for us to really begin to put the pieces together, as it were, to determine that there was a problem.

The beautiful simplicity of the faith we'd had in God initially was gradually being undermined. The message now being preached had a different edge to it.

Soon we were hearing what came to be called the "wilderness message." The point was that God was going to do a great work in us, to "purge out" our old, fallen nature and make us holy and fit for His use. Apparently, He could only do this as we "separated ourselves from the world system and its evil influences." Like the woman in the book of Revelation, we would be "hidden in the wilderness" (Revelation 12:6).

I resisted this message for some time, setting my focus on the good things I was hearing from other ministers. I knew that we were called to be a witness for Him *in* the world, not to be hidden away from it.

Many people were taking the plunge and launching out to the place the "father ministers" had "prepared" (picked out) for us in the wilderness of northern British Columbia.

Finally, I began to consider my own life, and as I did, I had to admit that there were many areas where I was falling short. I wasn't a very effective evangelist; I was too quiet and shy and didn't very easily witness to others. Come to think of it, my life didn't seem to be much of a testimony.

It was late fall of 1974, and I had been living in the house on Redpath Crescent for almost a year. I was still working full time at the pants factory on St. Lawrence Street, and I had just ended a relationship of three years. After I'd become a Christian, it seemed as though Devin and I had done nothing but argue every subject had sparked a debate. Of course, there had been others issues too, in both of our lives, that led to our going our separate ways.

By the following March, I was missing Devin and thinking in terms of new horizons in my life. So I succumbed to the idea that perhaps I did need a special work done in me to prepare and equip me for being a better Christian.

I didn't realize, as many Christians don't, that in Christ we have all we need to be a light to the world. No one told me that I didn't have to live under the dictates of the "old nature," or, as Paul called it, "the old man" (Ephesians 4:22–24).

CHAPTER 4

A Means to an End

"You can't get there from here."
author unknown

So, I was on my way to the "wilderness," the place where God would do a great work and change me into an effectual witness for Him.

There were three of us on that trip across Canada: Bob, who was the main driver, Cardamon, a dear friend from Montreal, and myself.

I met Cardamon at the church on University Street when I was still living in Chateauguay and commuting to work in Montreal. As a child, Cardamon had moved to Canada from Barbados with her parents. I remember visiting her home in Montreal and enjoying a delicious curry meal put together by her mother. Cardamon had moved into the big house on Redpath around the same time I had.

Bob had moved up from Buffalo, New York, to visit the group in Montreal, and a year or so later, he'd become engaged to my friend Dayna. I remember Dayna (in her mid twenties) bemoaning, in her funny and animated way, her apparent lot as a single woman. Looking in the mirror one morning, Dayna had wailed (half serious and half joking), "Oh, to be young and beautiful again! I'm almost thirty and destined to die as a lonely old maid."

Cardamon would just say, in her lovely Barbadian accent, "Dayna, Dayna, Dayna," and I'd try to talk sense to her. Dayna was actually beautiful, funny, and smart, and she'd had several relationships before moving to Redpath. When I mentioned this to her, Dayna replied, "Yes, sure, and here I am in a fellowship with so many options—single men under sixteen or over sixty-one."

Then one day, in walked Bob. Bob was tall and good-looking, a studious and somewhat pensive individual. But he possessed the rare quality of having a strong and confident foundation in the gospel of Jesus Christ. Even when the "fellowship" began to drift away from this simplicity, Bob stood firm, and I always admired him for that.

The leaders at the church in Montreal later accepted Bob as an elder, for they recognized his maturity. Then, when his preaching alluded to God's love and Jesus's provision as being pertinent and accessible for our present lives, he was called before the elders and told that his preaching was "first feast," meaning that it was only applicable for evangelism and was not suited for those on "higher spiritual levels, going on to perfection."

After three long days of driving, we were almost there. We had reached mile 143 up the Alaska Highway, north of Fort St. John, British Columbia. It wasn't much more than a post office, a general store, and a large motel and restaurant. I wondered who would ever frequent these facilities, which were set, it seemed to me, in the middle of nowhere.

There was an excitement in my heart about this new adventure, but strangely, there was also a deep, underlying sense of foreboding, perhaps partly because I felt that I was launching out into the unknown. As the car ascended one last hill, we stopped and paused for a moment to take in the sprawling panorama of sheer beauty and the wonder of God's creation. Mile upon mile of green, grassy patches mixed with golden hues among hills and valleys seemed to be tumbling over one another.

"Look!" shouted Bob, pointing across the way. "There's the farm." From our hilltop lookout, we could make out several little cabins, a few barns, a shop, and one larger log building (presumably the church). It was a little oasis of humanity hidden in the wilderness of British Columbia. Onward we continued, going down the next hill and following a winding, narrow road. We left the tarmac, bouncing and jostling over a pothole-peppered road for three miles, and then we were there. River Source Fellowship is what it was called.

Cardamon and I were to share a room in a tiny log cabin owned by a couple who both happened to be elders of the church. The room was about twelve by six feet. We were just able to fit a bunk bed along one wall and, on the adjacent wall, a night table and small dresser that belonged to Cardamon. The smallness of the room made it impossible for both of us to get up and dress at the same time.

We had arrived at the end of March, and summer didn't arrive until July. That first summer was unusually rainy, and in fact, the rain continued through June and July. Then we had a heavy frost overnight in mid July, and by September, summer was making its exit.

Those first few months found me painfully homesick for Montreal. I missed the long, hot summers, the lifestyle, and friends and family. One small consolation for me was the fact that my brother (and good friend) had already come to the community a year or so ahead of me. Our occasional talks were encouraging to me. Perhaps his previous experience there gave me a sense of continuity. Later on, our discussions became a kind of sounding board for me. I could elicit his feedback about my thoughts on particular messages that had been preached or issues that arose in my thinking—maybe to see if we were on the same page in our understanding.

October quickly ushered in winter, bringing with it shorter days and colder weather, with temperatures occasionally going down to -40°F. By November the sun came up around 11:00 a.m. and crept along the horizon until it was gone again by 4:00 p.m.

That first year, life was quite primitive. Cardamon and I learned the fine art of hauling in snow to melt on the stove for water. It was amazing how many buckets of snow it took to fill a barrel with water. As the snow melted, we'd pour it into a large barrel, which was conveniently placed beside the stove. In the spring, we'd have to sift the water through a cloth to remove the "wigglies" (mosquito larvae) that had made their nursery in our rain barrel outside.

In those days, kerosene lamps were the only source of lighting in our tiny cabin. Although they lent a cozy glow to the room and added to the inviting warmth of the wood stove, they did little to illuminate and were a challenge to read by. A year or two later, we got propane lighting, which turned out to be much more efficient, though it cost a little more.

Although winter was cold and the days were short, we often enjoyed clear skies and sunshine, which presented us with the vast beauty that surrounded us. Everywhere I turned, there was a painting waiting to be captured. At sunrise the mountains arrayed themselves in royal robes of purple and pink, shedding sparkling colors across the majestic landscape. When the temperature dipped down to -40°F, the atmosphere took on a crispness that amplified every sound. Voices echoed from one side of the valley to the other. Sometimes at night, the howl of wolves and the yelping barks of coyotes echoed across the valley.

In those early days of living in the community, I thought that maybe this experience of living a simple lifestyle separated from the distractions of the city—an experience I had resisted for some time in Montreal—was in fact, a good thing." I mused that perhaps God could use it to help people—including myself—to put off our Christian "personae," the religious masks we wore, and the roles we played. Perhaps this simple life could have some positive effect on our attitudes and relationships.

That first year found Cardamon and me very busy getting used to our new home with the couple to whom the little cabin belonged. We also gradually got acquainted with new people who had recently joined us: some from Portland, Maine, others from Oklahoma, and a few from Lubbock, Texas, and many other parts of the United States. As well, we reacquainted ourselves with old friends from the group from Montreal, who had left there before we had. And we were becoming familiar with the farm routine and schedules.

The schedule was necessary, in view of the many farm jobs and number of people, but it seemed to be the essence of the community. All the women were assigned to various jobs on a rotating schedule. Some of us worked in the garden a couple of times a week, while others were in the kitchen preparing meals. It was all very organized. We were divided into "kitchen teams" of three or four women, and there were about three teams, so we could alternate our schedules. These "teams" carried over into every area—working in the garden or greenhouse or doing whatever other jobs had to be done. My earlier musings on the benefits of a simple environment were losing their significance.

The heart of the community revolved around the large log building called the "tabernacle," a reference to a meeting place, not Moses's tabernacle. This massive structure really was an amazing endeavor, especially considering the fact that many of the builders there at the time had very little experience in building with logs. This fact was quite apparent in some of the earlier cabins, where logs had simply been laid down on the ground without any real foundation and, consequently, had rotted. Other logs in the buildings shifted through the seasons with the change of temperature, giving each cabin a kind of starboard list.

The tabernacle included a large dining room with space for meetings and church services. Massive log beams stood every twenty feet or so, supporting the second story. A heavy, barreled woodstove rested stately in the center, with a long pipe that reached its way through the second story and out to the chimney. The back half of the building contained the kitchen and pantry and, later, a milk room where we washed the milking utensils and kept a cheese press and butter churn. The second story held the schoolrooms and an office, which also accessed a loft where the stovepipe ran through, which was used for storage.

The kitchen, at times, could be a place of conflict, with personality clashes or differences of opinion. Everyone seemed to have her own particular way of doing just about anything. Still, there were some women who really enjoyed working together. Many different accents and manners of speech and expressions—not just from different parts of Canada or the States, but also having the multicultural aspect of Montreal—brought us the flavors of Mexico, Barbados, Jamaica, Italy, China, and Sri Lanka, which made for a wonderful mixture of expressions. In reference to how busy she was, one lady used to say, "I've been moving like I've been shot out of a cannon today!" Others said things like, "Just knead the bread, Honey. You don't have to beat it to death" or "This is the Eastern way of cooking."

For the first few years at River Source Fellowship, we had very little meat. Meals had to be pretty simple and innovative. Sometimes we had soybean patties as hamburgers. Later on, when we had a few chickens, some thrifty and creative individual produced gizzard pizza. Another time, we had "sloppy Joeys" over potatoes. Joey was a horse who had been getting on in years. He'd suffered the misfortune of a serious injury, which necessitated his retirement from work duties. Since we were desperate for meat, someone suggested Joey.

As the farm grew in population to about one hundred people, the programs also increased. We brought in more livestock—chickens, goats, horses, dairy cows, and beef cattle—which in turn necessitated working larger areas of land and planting hay, and that required tractors and equipment. We sold cattle and eggs, but soon it was necessary for some of the men to go out to work at logging and other jobs, some in Fort St. John and some in Dawson Creek and the surrounding areas.

One day as I was walking down the road from the cabins, I was alone for a moment and remembered my earlier thoughts. I had said to myself, "What a great opportunity, being out here, separated from the distractions of the city and job, and being able to spend some quiet time with the Lord, and studying the Word." Ironically, in this situation, finding time for such things had turned out to be even more of a challenge. The truth was that there was always some time off worked into the schedules, but time *alone* was not readily available, especially for a single person.

As singles, we were assigned to live with different families, and every year or two, we would be moved to another family. I got to know many people this way—adults and children—and some of the experiences were a special blessing. Others caused me to either seek God's help or just be miserable. It was a great blessing when the elders finally agreed to let single women share a cabin.

There were challenges, but for the most part, it was good. While living with a family, I'd always felt that I had to be doing something, helping in some way. As singles living together, we felt like equals. The best part was sharing our struggles, questions, or concerns, and even praying for one another. We had some fun times together too, and I learned to cross-country ski. I found a friend who was also an artist, and she and I often painted or sketched together. Often we went for walks.

Other scheduled jobs for the women included cleaning up the dining area and occasionally spending the morning eviscerating chickens. As the cattle program increased, we had the job of cutting up meat after a butchering, which necessitated a second day of boiling the bones and canning the broth.

Over every area of work there was assigned an overseer, who coordinated people and jobs and kept things going smoothly. Any decision that had to be made—like buying seeds for the garden, changing the feed for the goats, or moving someone to another team—had to go through the elders. If serious problems or conflicts occurred, the parties involved would often be called before the elders.

Occasionally I had my turn at that. "Margaret, you just need to submit," I was told emphatically by one elder.

"This is ridiculous," I said. "I've been working in this kitchen and making decisions in this area since before she even finished school. She's too young to be an overseer, and her arrogant attitude is not good for either her or myself."

"That's not the point," the elder told me. "You just have to learn to submit."

The young overseer really did have an attitude problem, and she seemed to carry an air of superiority about her. The fact was that I did have more experience than she did, but apparently, this wasn't the point.

"What *is* the point?" I said to myself later. As a young Christian— and maybe my perception was idealistic—I had assumed that we were there, having left our jobs and city life, so we could walk closer with God. I thought that perhaps, as a result, we'd grow in patience, peace, and wisdom, and in this way learn how to love one another. However, it appeared that this separated life had become all about performance and obedience to the rules. It may have looked good on the surface, but I wondered: was it producing Christian character or a change of heart?

On Sunday mornings at 10:00 a.m., we had a church service, which included a good time of praise and worship. Someone played the piano, and one or two played guitars, and the songs were good and encouraging. Some of the congregation would get up and share a song or poem, something the Lord had been saying to them during the week, or a scripture that was especially meaningful to them. Then we'd sit and listen to the messages preached.

There were about ten elders in all, and oftentimes three or four of them would share a message. During my first year of two in the community, the messages preached were often good and practical and applicable to our personal lives. They encouraged us to put our trust in God and to learn to seek His guidance in personal experiences. But in time, the emphasis began to change. The messages became all about submission and obedience. They were not so much about our personal lives as they were about the community, order, and our external performance—or so it seemed to me.

There was a lot of talk about "dying to self" but not as defined in scripture. It was as if every difficult situation (or person) we encountered was our "cross," and our submitting to it (or them) was "dying to self." Instead of working though problems, discussing the matter, and dealing with disagreements—for example, between elders or overseers and individuals—every conflict boiled down to obedience.

On Thursday evenings, we'd have a "tape night." (This was the eighties, and CDs hadn't yet come into general use.) At 7:00 p.m., we'd all make our way to the tabernacle and gather around the dining tables. It was a rather casual event, and many would bring with them some project to work on while listening to the tape. One man would be getting a haircut, while another repaired a saddle or a small piece of machinery. Some women would knit, and I'd sometimes do a bit of artwork. The tapes were generally from the "father ministers"—often Brother Stan—with messages taken from various conventions.

We continued attending conventions, even after moving to the farm community. Many people attended them, while some stayed back to maintain the farm duties.

One particular taped message, I remember, was taken from 1 Corinthians 11:3–10. In it, Brother Stan seemed to be typifying the ministers—which included the father ministers and the local church elders—as the "man" and the congregation—the rest of us—as the "woman." He pointed out the importance of what he called "covering," saying that the ministers were the "head" of the church. In view of this, we (the church) were obligated to submit to their leadership. Brother Stan explained it this way: "By learning to submit yourself to your covering [the elders, and so on], you are learning to submit to God."

After four years of living in the farm community, I began to notice a gradual change in people's attitudes. No longer was there any excitement about God, faith in Him, or the things He was doing in their hearts and lives. Instead, life was all about God's "dealings." Every difficulty—whether it was sickness, having to work on a particular schedule, or some conflict with another person—was considered a test, or trial, orchestrated by God with the purpose of purging out some aspect of the "sinful" carnal nature.

A popular saying was, "God is doing a work in me," which referred to some challenging situation or, in particular, one's reaction to that situation. If a person blew up in anger at another person, this phrase became a good excuse: "God is working some patience into me." But I never saw that patience actually manifested. On the farm, the phrase became almost a prideful response to going through some difficulty.

In the early days, we had enjoyed working together and rallying our resources to help one another, which we had done as a young church. But as time passed, things changed. The focus was on obeying rules and submitting to the "order."

Stan preached a message once on Ephesians 4:11, which speaks of God giving to the church apostles, prophets, evangelists, pastors, and teachers. Brother Stan presented it as though the list was in order of seniority, position, and authority (or rule). Of course, Stan called himself and the rest of the father ministers apostles. The local church elders were the pastors, whose role, I supposed, was to enforce the rule of the apostles. Stan called this hierarchy of rulership "God's divine order." This term slowly evolved to include the schedules and every area of the farm community, and eventually these things began to be called "the order" instead of, simply, the schedule.

One morning, Cardamon came to me looking very concerned. She said, "Margaret, Ron has been having a Bible study at his cabin, and some of the group from Montreal are attending. There are some serious issues that Ron has been studying, and he believes that the fellowship is in error."

At first I didn't realize the significance of what she was saying. I thought to myself, *So what? I've had a problem with some of the things Stan says, right from the start.* I had mentioned this to a few people, and all they'd said was, "Stan sometimes says extreme things just to get people's attention." Others would say, "God's Word is 'deep.' Maybe you don't understand it yet."

Then Cardamon added, "Ron's having a Bible study at his cabin this evening. Do you want to come?"

I did attend, and in some ways it took me back to those early days at Ron Wallace's Bible study on University Street. I witnessed to and agreed with much of what he was saying about brother Stan's message, but the underlying sense of arrogance among Ron's followers toward the rest of the fellowship angered me.

A week or so later, Stan Piper came to the River Source Fellowship, and a confrontation with Ron Wallace was arranged. We all gathered at the tabernacle to witness what came to be known as the "great debate."

Ron brought up many points, and Stan voiced his rebuttal. Back and forth it went for two hours. As right and clear as Ron's words were to me, I couldn't embrace them. I couldn't believe I felt this way, because I knew that what he was saying was right.

But I was appalled at the attitudes of those following Ron. Sitting behind me were some of those who had been attending Ron's "underground," as it were, Bible study. They were all sitting together, and they were laughing and ridiculing those seated across from them who had followed Stan and basically idolized him. Ironically, they themselves had continued in the fellowship for as many years. Some even heckled Stan as he talked. Had we lived in the 1500s, I'm sure they would have lynched him. The atmosphere was loaded with arrogance and a sense of condescension on the part of those on Ron's side.

One main point Ron brought up was, "You're teaching that we are trying to gain merit with God by becoming righteous through our works. We're already accepted and made righteous in Christ, and now our works overflow as a result of the fact that we are righteous.

Who has the final authority- the written Word or the Spirit?" Ron asked. "You're interpreting the Word by what you believe the Spirit is telling you."

Stan said, "The Holy Spirit teaches us and gives us revelation and understanding of the Word."

"But the written Word must be our reference," Ron said, "and it will confirm whether or not what we think we're hearing is true and in line with God's Word, the Bible.

So the debate ended, and within a few days, people began leaving the fellowship. Many of those who left with Ron were those who had been his admirers from the beginning, and, just like those who idolized Stan and hung on his every word, they looked up to Ron. Stan was in his forties or possibly early fifties, and Ron was in his thirties. The young people who had come to the Lord through Youth for Christ ministries had been in their teens or early twenties when they'd begun attending Ron's Bible studies, so he was a friend and mentor to many of them.

Some of those who left were good friends of mine, including my brother, Rick. Many who left continued to fellowship as a group with Ron in Fort St. John for a year or so. Others went their separate ways, returning to Montreal, the United States, and other places.

Rick told me later that he wasn't leaving with or because of Ron. He just felt that it was time for him to get on with other things. He thought that with so many people leaving, it was a good opportunity for him to make his move at that time. Rick moved down to Texas, where his then fiancée originated from. There they later married, and Rick started his own business as a cabinetmaker.

I continued in the fellowship for another four years, for I still wasn't convinced that the doctrine was entirely wrong. I had close friends who, in many ways, were in agreement with the fellowship's perspective. A few agreed with my questions but felt it unnecessary to make a full break. I still found encouragement in Bob Hall's preaching and that of a few others.

I was involved in the school, teaching a few classes. I had begun doing this shortly after my first year in the fellowship, and I thoroughly enjoyed this and loved the children. The routine of the farm community continued, and life went on. A few new people joined us, and that was good. Everything seemed to be all right. But the truth was, I was not.

After the Thursday tape night, I would go home troubled, wrestling with the many things being preached that I could not agree with. I discussed it with a few friends, but they thought it wasn't a big deal.

In June of 1986, I attended a convention. (I can't remember which one it was.) I remember sitting in the hall, and near the end of a long service, someone asked if we could pray for woman there who was crippled with arthritis and had been confined to a wheelchair for years. After some consideration, Brother Stan said, "Yes, we can pray for her." Then he continued, "But don't expect God to answer you until you are walking in complete obedience to 'the order' and are living righteously." He made no mention of faith in God or what is ours in Christ, only to "the order" and our obedience.

I was currently witnessing the results of this kind of teaching in the lives of women working in the kitchen, where the things we had once done joyfully, out of love, and with a sense of purpose had now become just something we were scheduled to do.

At that point, I stopped going to conventions altogether, mostly because of the sense of discouragement and fear it brought me. I was afraid that if these things they were preaching were true, I would never be good enough.

CHAPTER 5

Beginning of the End

"Come unto me, all who labor and are heavy
laden, and I will give you rest."
—Matthew 11:28

Through the years I spent in the fellowship, I carefully guarded my quiet time with the Lord. I'd often get up early in the morning, around 6:00 a.m., before trudging over to the tabernacle for breakfast. I'd get on my knees and just turn my attention on the Lord, remembering His faithfulness in my life since the time I'd become a new Christian and over my years in community. Whenever I felt discouraged or anxious or lonely, I'd return to that sense of His presence and find comfort.

As well, I recalled all the times the Lord had provided for me. Whenever I'd had a need, He had always provided. For example, one day I ran out of an item that young women frequently have need of, and I had no money coming in for the first few years on the farm to replace them. But I prayed about it, and the following day, an older woman approached me and handed me a small package of these unmentionables, saying that she didn't need them any longer and wondering if I could use them.

Another time, I wanted to visit my sister in Montreal, and I had no means of financing such a trip. I asked the Lord about it, and a day or two later, I found an envelope in my mailbox. I hadn't told anyone about this need, but in the envelope was a short note that said, "I just felt that the Lord wanted me to give this to you." It was more than enough money for plane fare to Montreal.

It became my habit to return to that place, or state of mind, and those times of refocusing and reawakening my faith in God kept me through many troubles.

I had stopped attending conventions, but I still continued going to tape nights and Sunday services. In spite of the many discrepancies, I continued in the fellowship for another years, specifically because of some responsibilities I had taken on.

Shortly after I'd moved to the farm, I'd been asked if I would teach an art class in the school. I wasn't a certified teacher, but I'd been approached because of my artistic abilities. I began with one small class of about eight students, and it evolved from there. It was so successful that I continued for ten years. I started out teaching one class of twelve-year-olds (seventh grade), and eventually I was teaching a class in every grade level, including one high school class. It was a small school in the fellowship, with about seventy students in all.

I was a good artist, but it was mostly raw talent. I'd never had any formal instruction, nor had I pursued art in a university. I began to realize that in order to teach art as a subject in school, I needed more than enthusiasm or personal ability. I realized that there were principles of perspective, color, and light and shadow, so I began some research. I found many helpful resources in bookstores in Fort St. John, and through the library. I had a friend who was also an artist and had taught art in the community. She was a great help and encouragement to me, and she shared some of her own ideas and resources so that I was able to develop an art curriculum for the school, one that other teachers have used.

Around the same time, there was a need for someone to teach a general knowledge Bible class to the elementary students. It was mainly historical and dealt with both the Old and New Testaments. I loved to study the Bible, and I discovered that I enjoyed teaching, so I volunteered.

Being that we were in such an isolated area, the school didn't have a lot of resources, so I also developed Bible class resources. I created my own lessons, charts, timelines, and so on, and at the request of the students, toward the end of every school year, we put on a play to illustrate some account we had studied. As well, I spent many hours putting up displays of my students' artwork. Although both art and Bible classes were part time, they required two or three hours, a few days a week. Taking into account all the hours of preparation, it occupied a large portion of my life at River Source Fellowship.

It was truly a gift and a great opportunity. I so enjoyed teaching and being involved with the students. It availed me with the opportunity to discover a capacity and passion that I would never have realized otherwise.

Weeks, months, and years passed, carrying with them a vast array of experiences, both good and bad, as well as developing some close friendships. Through the years though, the wrestling in my mind over doctrinal issues only increased. As time went on, I began to realize that there was truly some underlying error in the foundation of the fellowship. It was at that point that I began to set my attention on knowing with clarity what I believed—and in particular, what the scripture taught.

I committed myself to spending some time every day to draw near to God. Every evening after supper, I would return to my classroom where I could be alone with the Lord for a period of time. I had previously spent many hours there preparing lessons, so it was not unusual to see a light on in my classroom late into the night. At first I just got my guitar out, strummed the few chords that I knew, and just worshipped God, putting my focus on Him until something changed in my heart. Faith rose and peace returned, and before I realized it, an hour or two had passed as I rested in a stabilizing sense of His presence.

Whenever I had some free time, I'd study the Bible—especially the New Testament and the gospels in particular—to get a strong foundation in the new covenant. I got out my concordance and searched out the original Greek meanings of words in question. I immersed myself in the life and teachings of Jesus, as well as His death and resurrection. After all, Jesus came to show us what Father God is like and to teach and live out His will.

As I read the epistles and some of the Old Testament, I was able to understand them in view of this foundation. I also read several other books written by godly women and men through the centuries, especially people like John G. Lake, Smith Wigglesworth, and others.

Around this time, I was visiting my friend Dayna. One day in the course of the conversation, I mentioned my concerns. Dayna told me that her husband, Bob, had also recently been questioning the ministers' stands on certain issues. Bob and Dayna were considering leaving too.

Eventually, I began to realize that, although the fellowship ministry and I were saying some of the same words, we meant very different things.

I thought that the purpose of the fellowship—especially the farm community and the simple life—was about personal growth and maturity in walking with God and learning to know His voice and be led by His Spirit. I believed that dying to self was a personal matter that was to take place in the heart through the convicting work of the Holy Spirit. In this way, our focus would be on knowing God and His love. Only then could our lives and relationships prosper. This was the only foundation for an effectual church and witness to the world. I had assumed, at first, that everyone saw it this way.

I soon began to realize that the father ministers were focused on separating ourselves from the world in order to facilitate God's testing and dealings, with the purpose of purging out the sinful nature. This was to be accomplished by our submitting to a hierarchy of leadership with a focus on the "corporate man," a concept that I felt minimized a personal relationship with God. They believed that we were to find our strength, wholeness, and sense of identity in each other. This distorted concept of "dying to self" proved to be a self-centered version of the truth, as we focused on our performance, our obedience, and our efforts to change ourselves.

If the premise is wrong and the foundation faulty, eventually the whole structure will collapse. Even what little good may come out of it will be tainted. If the foundation of a building is a little off, then the builder will have to compromise along the way, adding an inch or so here and cutting a corner there, until the finished building is ugly and unstable.

It's very rare that a pastor would deliberately deceive or try to manipulate people, and this was not the case in the fellowship. If we relinquish our personal responsibility, we are training ourselves not to hear from God ourselves. We have to be discerning and know what we believe.

After the "great debate," my friend Cardamon—though she was still involved with the fellowship—had moved to Fort St. John and was working there. She had been hired as a social worker. Within a few years, after taking many related courses, she had her own office as a counselor. Someone had given her some tapes by James B. Richards, a pastor of a church in Alabama. She had benefitted from the tapes and had shared them with Beth, a mutual friend of ours at River Source. I had met Beth and her sister Hymie briefly at the church in Montreal. They had just immigrated from Sri Lanka and later moved up to the fellowship in northern British Columbia. There we shared a small cabin, and over the years we became good friends.

Cardamon had suggested that Beth pass the tapes on to me, but after hearing them, Beth had apparently been reluctant to do so, fearing that they would solidify my decision to leave.

I did eventually listen to them, and she was right. For me, they were life changing. In one message, Pastor Jim spoke of God's love and how greatly He values us. He clearly laid out the fact that we are righteous and accepted by God—just as the apostle Paul taught in his letter to the Romans—not by our own efforts or merit but as a result of all that Jesus accomplished for us through His death, burial, and resurrection. Pastor Jim's words reawakened my heart and mind to the simplicity of faith and the trust I'd had in God at the beginning.

After this, I went for many long walks with a tape deck in my pocket and earphones in my ears, reestablishing my heart in the truth of this new covenant. It was time to leave the fellowship. I could no longer live in an environment that contradicted my own convictions. It was truly amazing how—when I began to trust God and my ability to hear and then stepped out in faith—things began, little by little, to fall into place.

After fourteen years of living at River Source Fellowship, I found myself faced with a choice: I could live in regret for having wasted a big chunk of time under a wrong premise, or I could thank God for the amazing opportunities and experiences it had afforded me, as well as the precious and dear friends that I had gained. More than anything else, it was through my many experiences (and sometimes in spite of them) that I learned to lean upon the Lord and found His unfailing love and faithfulness.

In considering the move, it was my intention to find work and eventually return to Quebec. But this idea never felt right, as so many things had changed for me in Montreal. Finally, I decided to move to a small town called Smithers, that was a twelve hour drive south of Fort

St. John. I had visited Smithers once while on a trip to Los Angeles, California, about four years prior to my move, and I did like the area.

I lived in Smithers for about a year, during that time I got a job as a cook's helper at A&W (a job I endured for about a month). Then I found employment as a "support worker," taking care of people with mental challenges. I found it challenging and it taught me to care. Finally, I found a job as an ESL tutor, teaching English as a second language. I enjoyed it so much that I took a course so I could be a better teacher/tutor, and I still do this part time.

It was during my first year in Smithers that I met the man to whom I am now very happily married. It would fill another book to share the many good things the Lord has done and continues to do in my (now *our*) life as I continue to lean on Him.

I'm not sharing these things simply to tell my story or to prove a point or win an argument. My purpose is to give honor to God and to affirm to you His goodness and faithfulness. For the remainder of this book, I will unfold for you some of what I have learned—partly through this experience—and especially what I have come to realize regarding what this Christian life is really meant to be.

CHAPTER 6

What Really Is a Normal Christian Life?

*If we don't know what we're looking for, how
will we know when we find it?*
M. Belanger

I've been a Christian now for about forty years, and it's only within the past few years that I have been able to answer this question with peace and confidence.

After leaving the fellowship, I had the opportunity to attend and be part of several different churches over the years, and it's true that I have benefitted in some way from each one. Still, I have carried with me this lingering question: what really is a normal Christian life?

Sadly, in spite of all the good things in many churches I attended, I found that there continued to be within me a sense that something vital was missing. For some time, I wasn't able to pinpoint or articulate exactly what that was. Discovering the answer was a gradual process that covered several years of soul-searching, deliberation, study, and prayer—and of course, just getting on with life, family, and friends.

But little by little it became clear to me exactly what God intends our lives as believers to be. Above and beyond everything else, the Christian life is about a relationship—a fact so obvious and so simple that we often miss it. It's so easy to slip into the cultural lifestyle of a "Christian," and in our busy lives we lose sight of what being a Christian is really all about.

I saw lots of good programs: women's ministries, Bible studies, prayer chains, cell groups where we encouraged and prayed for one another, and youth ministries where young people went out on the streets or to other countries to serve people in need and share with them about God's love. These were great things. I loved to hear about them and even be involved myself, and I heard many inspiring messages. But as good as it all was, I still felt as though something was missing.

During my search, I also read a few books written by or about people whose lives not only demonstrated the reality of what they believed, but showed that something far greater was behind their good works. The inspiration that motivated them, and the effectual power that worked in them, did not come entirely out of their own natural resources and capabilities. This capacity was a reflection of a relationship with God. This is not to say that the rest of us don't seek God, His will, and His help, but this relationship has to be more than a simple "tell us what to do, and we'll do it" or "grant us the strength to do this." We need *Him* to inspire and empower us.

The other day when I picked up the mail, I found an advertisement for a Christian DVD series that I could order. The advertisement outlined some of the topics that were covered. It focused on "the things that Jesus said and taught," and it spoke of things like "taking care of the poor," "finding justice for the oppressed," "loving one's enemies," and "spreading the good news." All these things are good, and we all want to be (and should be) doing such things. Thousands of sermons and Sunday morning services are centered around these very topics. But the truth is that this cannot be the Christian's primary focus. Sometimes we become so involved in doing these good things that we lose sight of our premise and the one we are seeking to serve.

A few years ago, I was watching the funeral of Jack Layton, former leader of the NDP party in Canada. Reverend Brent Hawkes, a friend of Mr. Layton, led the service. He was a good speaker, and he was clear in what he shared: that Jack Layton was a good man who had valued and genuinely cared for others. Mr. Layton had lived in a way that reflected his convictions, even though he wasn't a Christian. Reverend Hawkes quoted Jack as often saying things like "working together for common good" and "making this world a better place is up to us."

The service ended with a song that I remember from the early seventies, "Get Together" by The Youngbloods. It spoke of wars and various injustices in the world at that time, and it ended with a line that went something like this: "Come on, everybody, smile on your brother; let us love one another, right now."

It all sounds so good, and we as Christians aspire to such benevolence. The problem is that without God inspiring, directing, and empowering us in a personal way, it's nothing but "humanistic socialism." Sometimes I wonder if we really know the difference.

The problem with humanism is that it's humanity-based and not God-based. It puts mankind at the center of everything, like the citizens of Babel whose power was in their unity. They said, in essence, "Together we can do anything." They found their strength and inspiration in each other. There are all kinds of human endeavors that have accomplished many things. Even if the people involved don't acknowledge God, He has blessed them with minds to learn and to create. When our focus is on good works, we become motivated by needs instead of being led by the guidance of the Holy Spirit.

Humanism, in many ways, is the opposite of Christianity. We have a source beyond ourselves. Our inspiration, direction, and empowerment to do things comes from Him and springs forth out of our relationship with Him. Christianity is not a social network, a friendship club, or even a charitable organization, for our good works must only be a reflection of knowing Him. We might be coworkers together in this world, but each of us must find our source in Him.

In the fellowship, we were taught to think of ourselves together as one "corporate person," forgetting that it's only through a personal connection with Him that we have anything to offer in a church context. We can encourage and counsel one another, but in our weaknesses, we cannot ultimately be the true source of strength for each other. We can only point one another to Christ. A corporate mentality can only lead to codependence, because only God can be our source. God relates to us as individuals, and only in this personal, intimate way can He work through us.

In the days of the early church, some groups had all things common. They supported one another financially and shared their food and housing. They encouraged one another, prayed for each other, and ministered healing one to another. But they were not disciples of one another. They were followers of Jesus. He was their source of inspiration, motivation, and direction. He taught them and encouraged their faith, and later He empowered them. So it is, and must be, the responsibility and privilege of each one of us to connect with God as our personal source.

Socialism, on the other hand, is similar in some ways to the thinking of the fellowship, in that all things were provided and decided for us. In socialism, everyone, per se, is equal, but unfortunately this often equates to being equally *poor*. This might eliminate the gap between wealthy business owners and those in abject poverty, but when everything is done corporately and for the community, we find that people are robbed of personal responsibility, as well as initiative and enterprise. We were designed to use and develop our personal gifts, imagination, and creativity. Enterprise and responsibility cause people to thrive. Socialism, or corporate living, may look good in some ways, but it's not God's way.

So, what is this Christian life really about? Some churches I've attended have made social programs and evangelism their main focus. Others seem to have focused on correct doctrine, and they are very knowledgeable about theology, guarding their views from the slightest deviation from what orthodoxy allows. Still others set their hearts on the gifts and the power of the Holy Spirit.

Is the Christian life about performance or acting a certain way? Is it about just being and doing good? Is it about holiness and sinlessness or God's dealings toward this end? Is it about following rules and laws? Is it about doing the best we can while we're here? Is it about waiting for heaven or waiting for God to do something?

What is a normal Christian life really about?

It's so easy to become centered on good works or any of the many varying church priorities, but even though these things are valid and necessary, we can't let them become our reason for being. If our focus is solely on our good works, we'll be no different from good nonbelievers. If we're not careful, our Christianity will simply become part of our Christian culture. We will do certain things just because that's what Christians do, or we will do things a certain way just because that's how we've always done it. If we allow our church priorities to become our main focus, we'll miss the simplicity of the gospel.

Many of our Christian efforts and good works are commendable, and many of our church programs are good and beneficial for ourselves and others. But there is really only one priority in this Christian life. The focus of every serious, blood-bought, redeemed believer has to be on knowing God in a personal way and growing in that relationship. Only then will we truly find the capacity to live this life, and only in this way can our works be truly empowered and effective.

CHAPTER 7

Propensities and Modus Operandi

"There is a way that seems right unto a man, but
the end thereof is the way of death."
—Proverbs 16:25

When we first come to Christ, we feel clean and at peace, and we know that we are forgiven and accepted. We read the Bible, and we see God's promises and good will for us, and we enter this new life full of hope and expectation.

Gradually, it all seems to fade. Sometimes this is due to our church or denominational perspective. Or perhaps a well-meaning pastor who is zealous for a virtuous church begins to turn our attention on our sins and our failures—assuming, I suppose, that this will cause us to repent and seek God.

Oftentimes our circumstances draw us away from that first hope and expectation as we consider the many problems in our lives: financial difficulties, a failing marriage, children who are not living our Christian ideals, and so on. All these things can cause us to focus on ourselves and our shortcomings instead of on God's Word, provision, and promises.

Then we begin the arduous task of trying to change ourselves. We all want to live a godly life and be pleasing to God, but soon we find that our efforts are not enough. We're not always consistent, and we're often tempted and prone to go off track. Our faith wavers as we confront our own limited capacity to live this Christian life.

In the fellowship church, a big part of our lives and perspective involved submission to the rules ("the order") and the elders. People believed that in this way they could change themselves. They believed that through this kind of self-denial, suffering, and difficult situations our sinful tendencies would be "purged out of us."

We were like the Pharisees of Jesus' time began with a sincere desire to please God and keep all the laws, but it wasn't long before our focus turned to our efforts and performance. As it was with them, our performance could only produce self-righteousness and pride—or contrariwise, the condemnation of falling short. And perhaps we, like the Pharisees, resorted to greater performance after our failures, attempting all the more to give an appearance of holiness.

At River Source Fellowship, it started with a few rules we had to abide by. There was nothing wrong with that, per se, but little by little the rules (the "order") almost became an end in themselves. For example, at the beginning there was a certain dress code for women. In view of decency and moral standards, women had to wear skirts, never pants. While I was in Montreal, I remember Stan Piper saying, "Pants on women causes them to act masculine." Then the elders established an acceptable length: two finger widths below the knee. Some women were even called before the elders for wearing skirts that were considered too short.

This dress code continued on the farm, where women were required to wear skirts even while working in the garden. Occasionally some of us would go picking wild berries, which was a little awkward in a skirt, and some women wore pants under their skirts. Ironically, while the skirt regulations continued, a little indiscretion behind a barn resulted in a young girl finding herself pregnant. The rules really didn't change anyone.

On the farm, certain times were set up for meals, meetings, and schedules, which, of course, was a reasonable arrangement. But as time went on, people occasionally arrived late, and then a thee next church service they were reprimanded. The occasional tardiness wasn't so much a problem, but the main issue became "submission to the order." This may sound like a trivial matter, but the truth is that after the "great debate" and many people leaving, there came a spiritual lull among those who chose to stay. People began coming late to meals, work schedules, and church services, or they didn't bother to come at all. This often tends to be the outcome when we try to regiment godly living.

Requiring people to follow certain rules can be helpful, but in a sense, it can rob us of personal responsibility to hear from God ourselves. Sometimes it seems easier to do what we are told than it is to seek God ourselves to know what He wants us to do. All our legalistic efforts in the fellowship couldn't change anyone. Taking personal responsibility involves being honest with ourselves and seeking God to affect the change.

Sometimes behavior modification through submitting to man-made regulations can give us a false sense of security. We think that as long as we're performing, we must be all right. Then, left to ourselves and faced with a temptation or challenge, whatever is in our hearts comes flooding to the surface, because nothing has changed in our hearts.

After leaving the fellowship and attending other churches, I soon realized that these concepts were not unique to the fellowship. I haven't seen many overt control tactics in churches, but on a personal level, there are some subtle ways by which we try to make ourselves right with God or better Christians—or perhaps, in some way, more acceptable.

I've seen it in my own life. I attended a church (not the fellowship) where we were encouraged to get involved in some of its many programs. They said, "Find an area that God wants you to be involved in!" Personally, I didn't feel an inclination toward any of the many areas at the time. But I felt the pressure and recognized that there was a need for people to get involved.

So I jumped in and volunteered to help in the children's church on Sunday mornings. Later, another need came up. The children's ministry was asking for more people to help with AWANA, an evening kids' program that focused on evangelism by helping kids memorize Bible verse. So I got involved in that too. I even helped with decorating for a women's Christmas retreat. All these things were good, and it's right to do our part, but besides feeling exhausted, I started feeling like I was really something and proud of it.

Then one day I found myself resenting those who weren't doing as much as I was. My attitude wasn't good, so eventually I stopped some of the things I was involved in. Then I started feeling guilty. Finally, I had to ask myself, "Am I doing these things for the acceptance of others? Am I trying to find greater acceptance from God by my efforts?" These weren't trivial, inconsequential questions. They were the basis, if only partially, for my motives.

Someone once told me that he had a problem with bad thoughts. He said that in order to keep his mind on God and keep his mind pure throughout the day, he had begun to memorize scriptures. He even tried to think about God all day. He soon grew weary of this, or sometimes he got distracted, and before he knew it, the old thought patterns were back in operation. The harder he tried, the wearier he got. All this "sin management" might help for a while, but we cannot change ourselves this way.

I've read accounts of godly men and women living centuries ago who attempted to live aesthetic lives, separating themselves from the "world," subduing their natural propensities, and even denying their basic needs in order to produce holiness. Have you ever noticed that the religious paintings of that time depicted angels, various "saints," and even Jesus as ethereal and void of emotion? This was intended to portray an appearance of holiness, of being disconnected or unaffected by the evil desires of the world.

None of the things we do can make any of us holier. Our efforts will never do the job.

Sometimes, when all else fails, we cry out to God to change us. A few years ago, my husband and I were attending a "revival service" in a particular church. Some people were kneeling at the altar, which I too have done at times. They were sincere, godly people reaching out to God in fervent, earnest prayer, pleading with God to move in their lives in greater ways.

As the service progressed, the singing and shouting increased in volume. Some people were banging drums, others were waving flags, and some were crying and wailing, imploring the Spirit to fall upon them. "Fall upon us now, Holy Spirit, and break our hardened hearts," they pleaded. "Give us a heart to love, and make us holy and righteous and pleasing to You."

There certainly is a valid need for us to seek God earnestly, and He promised that He will be found by us if we seek after Him with all our hearts. I'm not trying to belittle what was going on when I say that— after an hour or two of their banging drums, shouting, and begging God—I felt as though I was amongst the prophets of Baal, who cried and cut themselves to get their god to respond.

Many churches are unfamiliar with this type of service, but the truth is that we all do these things in our own (though perhaps more subtle) ways. We beg God and try to impress Him with our earnestness, and in this way we attempt to manipulate Him to move on our behalf. We want Him to zap us with a great anointing that will instantly break our hardened hearts and change us. We want Him to make us more loving, motivated, and empowered, and to give us a passion for the lost.

These are all valid desires, but there is something missing in this kind of prayer. When we pray this way, we are, in fact, inadvertently denying what Jesus has already done for us through His death, burial, and resurrection. We read about it in the Bible, but we somehow forget—or perhaps we never really understood—what Jesus has already done for us. Our hearts cannot grasp the magnitude of His love or the all-sufficiency of His provision.

When our efforts and pleading don't seem to afford the change we desire, we may tell ourselves—if we're not careful, and contrary to scripture—that surely these things—like holiness, righteousness, empowerment, and victory—cannot be possible for us in this earthly life. So we continue to struggle with failure, lack, and many kinds of limitations that mar our testimony, and we accept them as a normal part of life.

Whether they are the church's rules and disciplines, our personal efforts, or even our earnest desires and begging prayers, we cannot change ourselves, nor can we manipulate His response. But thank God, He has a better way. His way is complete, effectual, and lasting, and Jesus has already wrought it for us.

Ironically, in this day, it appears that the things that stand in the way of our experiencing authentic Christian life and personal change are the very things that stood in opposition to the truth and life that Jesus brought us when He came to earth.

CHAPTER 8

Dogs, Crumbs, and the Law

"The law itself is good and offers us safety and benefits;
but as new covenant believers we cannot
relate to God through the law."
—Author unknown

In Mark 7:24–30, we see Jesus and His disciples at the borders of Tyre and Sidon, entering a house to find solitude from the crowds. In essence, this is what happened, as I see it. A Greek, Syrophoenician woman had heard that Jesus was there, and she came to the house. With no introduction or formality, she simply ran to Jesus, crying, "Have mercy on me, O Lord, Son of David! My daughter is oppressed of a devil."

Jesus seemed to ignore her. The disciples suggested that he send her away because she was not a Jew. But she fell on her knees before Him and continued to plead all the more.

"But Jesus said to her, 'Let the children be filled first, for it is not good [appropriate] to take the children's bread and throw it to the little dogs" (Mark 7:27 NKJV).

I used to cringe when I read this scripture, until I realized that even though God saw the problem and cared, and Jesus had come to bring a new covenant of hope for all, He had not yet suffered on the cross or made available full salvation through His resurrection. He had been sent first to the Jews, and he had to relate to them through the Law, which was their means of relating to God at that time.

Showing no sign of being offended, she answered Him, "Yes, this is true, Lord [affirming that she was not a Jew and was not a partaker of the Jewish covenant], "yet even the dogs under the table eat from the children's crumbs."

"But Jesus answered and said to her, 'Oh woman, great is your faith! Let it be to you as you desire.' And her daughter was healed from that very hour" (Matthew 15:28 NKJV).

Through simple faith, this woman was able to reach beyond the limits of the Law. This was inconceivable in view of the old covenant.

It's true that Jesus Himself had grown up under the Law, and as a Jew, he had studied the scriptures and kept all the feasts. Yet during his earthly ministry, He spoke of things that far surpassed the Law.

Looking into the Law a little further in Deuteronomy 5:1, we see Moses presenting the commandments to Israel. "And Moses called all Israel, and said to them, 'Hear, O Israel, the statutes and the judgments which I speak in your ears this day, that you may learn them, and keep, and do them.'"

For centuries, the Jews had lived under the Law and all that it entailed. In Deuteronomy 6:7, Moses exhorted Israel regarding the laws and precepts when he said, "And you shall teach them diligently unto your children, and shall talk of them when you sit in your house, and when you walk by the way, and when you lie down, and when you rise up." The law permeated every part of their lives.

"Then it shall come to pass, because you listen to these judgments and keep and do them that the Lord your God shall keep with you the covenant and the mercy which He swore to your fathers ... He will love you and bless you and multiply you: he will also bless the fruit of your womb, and the fruit of your land, your corn, and your wine, and your oil, the increase of your cattle ... Thou shall be blessed above all people ... and the Lord will take away from you all sickness" (Deuteronomy 7:12-15 NKJV)

Many Jews who kept the Law experienced these benefits and promises. As long as they continued therein, they prospered. But as generations passed, the heart of the principles was lost, for they settled into tradition.

In the fellowship, the more we focused on submitting to the rules, the greater the apathy. Soon the reason and original inspiration were forgotten. This same attitude occurred among the Pharisees, the Jewish leaders in Jesus's day, as little by little, their keeping of the laws became simply an outward show and religious performance. Their hearts became dull, and they lost sight of the loving intent of the one behind the laws and principles.

Let's consider "the Law" for a moment, but before we do, let's start from the beginning to give us some background.

In Genesis, we read that mankind "walked with God" (Genesis 2:1–15), and all their needs were met. They were happy, healthy, intelligent, beautiful, and completely innocent. They had no concept of evil. There was no guilt, no shame, no pain, and no sickness or lack—or any of the many negative things that we experience today and consider normal.

It was apparent that God's intent for mankind was only good. There was no law, just a relationship—a loving, trusting relationship that was the basis for their lives.

We know that man was given a free will from the beginning, for love can only function through choice. Love does not demand or coerce; you cannot force someone to love or trust you.

We also know that in the Genesis account, man chose amiss and consequently fell from the place of blessing that was his while he remained in relationship with God, his source.

It wasn't until several generations later, in Moses's day, that the law was given (Deuteronomy 5–6). In a real sense, the law and all its principles and values are a reflection of the very heart of God: His character, wisdom, care, goodness, and good will for us.

The law was given for the people's good, "that it may be well with you and your children" (Deuteronomy 4:40). It had immediate benefits, which included: healthy dietary principles, wisdom for success and prosperity, and direction for cooperation, peace, and stability. Staying within the law's bounds gave them a perimeter of protection.

With the law came the possibility of "blessings" or "curses" (Deuteronomy 7:12–15; 28:1–14). If Israel would live in accordance with the principles of the law, then they would experience health, prosperity, and many other blessings. Scripture tells us that they would flourish and succeed in "all that they put their hands to do."

However, if anyone departed from the principles of wisdom, all of their efforts would eventually fail, and troubles and calamity of all kinds would ensue (Deuteronomy 28:45–61). Living under the parameters of the law made possible a degree of access and acceptance with God. Until Jesus came, the law and sacrifices were the only means by which people could approach God.

The Israelites defined the issue well when they said regarding the keeping of the law (the Ten Commandments) that "it shall be our righteousness, if we do these things" (Deuteronomy 6:25). Under the law, everything depended on man's efforts and abilities. As I have witnessed in Christian community, laws and rules can be useful, but if our confidence and sense of acceptance with God rests on our keeping the laws, we miss the point.

When we think of "the law," we tend to think only in terms of the Ten Commandments, even though there were many more precepts and principles. But in the Old Testament times when "the law" was spoken of, it represented a whole system of thought, lifestyle, and culture. It was the premise upon which people based their whole perspective on life and the way they lived. Children grew up memorizing the scriptures, and their parents diligently spoke to them of the laws and principles, which they had been commanded to do (Deuteronomy 6:7). As well, they regularly rehearsed the historic accounts of Israel. The life of the Jew revolved around the feast days, which coincided with the planting and harvesting of their crops as recorded in the laws.

It's funny—in the sense of "strange"—and sad, even today in this New Testament time since Jesus has come, that some of us still tend to look to the law or our good works to merit favor with God. Within many churches today, we can see the law as a cultural paradigm in subtle ways. I've heard well-meaning preachers present from the pulpit the principles that Jesus taught as though they were simply more rules and laws for us to perform. I've sat under preachers who have taken Matthew 5, for example, and presented some of the truths therein as more laws.

I recently heard one pastor say, "In this New Testament time, we must realize that much more is required of us. Jesus made it clear that we have to obey God's laws, not only in our deeds but also in our thoughts and attitudes." This is true, in a sense, but if our focus is still on our performance (our good works), we become like the man I mentioned earlier who was striving not to think evil thoughts. Instead of setting his attention on Jesus and what He has done for us, he was laboring to change his thinking.

We're like the dogs eating the crumbs that fall from the table, when in fact (in the new covenant) we are His children, adopted into His family, and we have access to so much more. When we first accept Jesus as Lord and Savior, we give up our efforts to try to change ourselves. For there is birthed within us, a realization that we are forgiven and accepted, and we are a new and righteous creation in Him.

It's hard to be a good Christian by our own efforts. Keeping the law can only produce the outward appearance of right living; it cannot change our hearts. The law looked forward to the time when it would be fulfilled through Christ.

Jesus said, "Unless your righteousness exceeds the righteousness of the scribes and Pharisees, you will by no means enter the kingdom of heaven" (Matthew 5:20 NKJV). He wasn't laying down more rules requiring greater effort. Instead, He was pointing people to something better. Jesus didn't come to destroy the law but to fulfill it (Matthew 5:17). Jesus fulfilled—that is, satisfied and completed—the law through His life, death, and resurrection, and He is now in us (by His Spirit).

Because of Jesus, my righteousness is no longer dependent upon my good works or keeping the law. Paul said to the Galatians, "If my righteousness comes by law, then Christ is dead in vain" (Galatians 2:21). For Christ came that this righteousness would be in us as a real part of us.

In his letter to the Philippians, Paul wrote that he wanted "to be found in Christ, not having my own righteousness, which is of the law, but that which is through the faith of Christ, the righteousness of God by faith" (Philippians 3:9).

He also said, "Christ is the end of the law for righteousness [the law as a means of attaining righteousness] to everyone who believes."

Isaiah speaks of a time when we shall "be established in righteousness." *Righteousness* means "rightness, rectitude, justification, virtue, or prosperity". The Hebrew word is taken from a root word that means "morally or legally clean." Because of Jesus, our righteous standing before God is a settled matter. Isaiah then goes on to say that this righteousness is our "heritage," because in Christ we are adopted into His family as sons and daughters.

Our righteousness is not the result of our obedience to the law. It is not like Israel's confession to Moses when they said (in reference to their keeping the laws), "This shall be our righteousness." No! We are righteous because we are now in Christ, and He is our righteousness. Jeremiah spoke of this very fact when he prophesied that Jesus would be called "the Lord our righteousness" (Jeremiah 23:5–6).

The world into which Jesus first came was a culture steeped in the law, but when He returns, He'll be looking for something more than law-keepers.

CHAPTER 9

New Wine and New Wineskins

"And the light shines in the darkness and the
darkness did not comprehend it."
John 1:5

During my time in the Christian community, I came to believe that God's dealings in my life worked toward one main end: my sinlessness, holiness, and righteousness. A big part of this perspective was based on the old covenant premise that God is holy and cannot tolerate sin. Very little was said about the fact that God, as well as being holy, is love and that Jesus came and dealt with the sin issue.

Many Christians, I have discovered, also hold to this kind of thinking to some extent. They live—as I did for some time—under various degrees of condemnation, never really knowing with any confidence God's estimation of them. Sadly, in some churches I have attended, I've found that many Christians, even today, believe that this walk with God is primarily about obedience to His laws.

I've heard Christians, when faced with a sickness or some kind of tragedy or loss, say, "What did I do wrong?" or "Why is God punishing me this way?" After attending a promising job interview only to discover that the position had already been filled, a Christian friend of mine said, "God must want to humble me," and then added, "He is dealing with my pride." I've heard someone commenting on another person's difficulty as "the hand of God."

As a young Christian in the fellowship, I sometimes found myself in a kind of a dilemma after doing something I shouldn't have done or saying something I shouldn't have said—or contrariwise, after not doing something I *should* have done or not saying something I *should* have said. Afterward, I'd be under condemnation. It sounds ridiculous, but if we're living under the law, what assurance do we have?

Jesus came into the world as a Jew. He grew up in a Jewish culture and began His ministry among Jews, but His words spoke of things beyond their comprehension, far exceeding their prevailing dogma. His message reached far beyond the rudiments of the law and extended to all mankind. Yet His people shut their ears to His words and hardened their hearts to His counsel.

John told us that "in Him was life" and this "life was the light of men." He went on to say that this "light shines in the darkness and the darkness doesn't comprehend it."

Interestingly, the word *comprehend* in the original Greek means much more than "to understand," which I had always assumed. It actually means "to take eagerly," that is, "to grasp, seize, lay hold on, or possess."

In the darkness of the hearts and reasoning of the people in John's day, they didn't recognize the light as something desirable, and they had no incentive to go after it, to reach out and take it into their hearts and lives. They didn't "eagerly lay hold on" what a loving God was offering them. Even today, we're afraid to imagine that God is in fact good and that He always has intended more for us than simply obedience.

Despite their calamity of soul and body—living in a state of separation from their source of true light, blessing, and provision—the Jews clung to the darkness of their own understanding. They thought they were rich, erudite, and wise. Jesus saw them as "sheep without a shepherd" (Matthew 9:36). Looking over Jerusalem, He wept, for it was not as it should, or could, have been.

There was a time when Jesus's followers came upon a man who had been blind from birth. They asked Jesus, "Who sinned, this man or his parents, that he was born blind?" (John 9:2 NKJV). They were speaking from their perspective of being under the law, the old covenant. They assumed that someone must have violated the law for such a calamity to befall someone.

In essence, Jesus said, "This is an opportunity for God and His goodness to be made apparent. While it is day, and I have the opportunity, I work the works of God." This is the implied meaning of the original language.

King James version says it this way, "Jesus answered, 'Neither this man nor his parents sinned. But that the works of God should be revealed in Him. I must work the works of Him who sent me while it is day; the night is coming when no one can work. As long as I am in the world, I am the light of the world'."

Jesus was deeply concerned and always had compassion on the sick and troubled. He marveled at their unbelief and grieved over their hardness of their hearts, for they were more concerned with the keeping of the law than with compassion.

One day, Jesus went into a synagogue, and there was a man with a withered hand (Matthew 13:15). The Pharisees were watching Him to see whether he would heal someone on the Sabbath (Mark 3:5 AB). He glanced around at them with vexation and anger, grieved at their hardness of heart, and He healed the man. Then Jesus said to them, "This people's hearts are calloused, and their ears are dull. They have closed their eyes in case they might see the light, grasp the truth, understand with their hearts, and be converted and change their thinking. I would heal them." But as Isaiah once said, "They would not."

On another occasion, Jesus and his disciples were picking and eating grain from a field. The Pharisees were once again watching and accused them of breaking the Sabbath by picking grain, which was considered a form of work. Jesus answered by saying, "The Sabbath was made for man and not man for the Sabbath." We could also say, in the same light, that man was not made for the law, but the law was made for man. It was given for our benefit, and we are not its servants.

Jesus called God "Father" (John 5:18) and spoke of a relationship available to all. He exercised authority and demonstrated power. He forgave the sins and healed the diseases even of sinners (Luke 5:18–24). Jesus taught and demonstrated things far beyond their "law" mentality. For many, there was a veil (as Paul later described it) over their hearts (2 Corinthians 3:15). Many were offended by the things He said and did.

So intent were the Pharisees on keeping the law and taking pride in their efforts that they laid law upon law, and stipulations that went far beyond the requirements of the law. They held to the structure, the form and the scaffolding, but they missed the purpose and loving intent behind it all.

They found fault with everything Jesus said and did, because it didn't fit into their preconceived, inflexible perceptions. In answer to their constant confuting, Jesus said to them, "No one puts new wine into old, worn-out wineskins, because the new wine, as it expands, will burst the skins, and the wine will be spilled and the skins be destroyed. New wine must be put into new wine skins, and then both are preserved" (Luke 5:37–38, paraphrased).

Jesus brought a whole new paradigm, a new way of seeing, thinking, and living.

Directing light onto an object brings us greater insight into its design and purpose. In science, we often consider a matter and come to a hypothesis with limited understanding, but upon further examination—when greater light is shed on a subject, or we view it from another angle—we can then see with a broader perspective and understand in a greater, clearer way. So it is with God's Word and reality.

Jesus, continuing his illustration, said to the Pharisees, "No man, also having drunk old wine, immediately desires the new, for he says, 'The old is better'" (Luke 5:39, paraphrased).

Sometimes it's difficult for us to let go of our old perceptions and opinions, especially when it comes to scripture and doctrinal views. When we are used to seeing things a certain way for some time, it's hard to accept a fresh view. We hold to what is comfortable and familiar, even when it doesn't produce what we had hoped it would.

In the fellowship, I lived for many years under a particular perspective and view of the scriptures. Although I saw that there was some error, that perspective had become familiar to me, and for some time I was afraid to leave. When I began listening to the tapes of Pastor Jim Richards, I witnessed the fact that what he said was true, and my own study of the scriptures confirmed what he was saying. Yet it took me a few years, even after leaving the fellowship, before the truth could get from my head and intellect to my heart—where I was finally able to confidently trust God and His Word and to live it and share it.

Hearing God's Word, comprehending His love, and taking hold of it in our lives requires so much more than laws and mere understanding. We must come to Him as children, in simple faith and trust.

CHAPTER 10

The Good News

"As cold water to a weary soul, so is good news from a far country."
—Proverbs 25:25

An angel appeared to some shepherds who were tending their sheep. They were terrified at the encounter, but the angel said to them, "Do not be afraid, for behold, I bring you good tidings of great joy, which will be to all people. For there is born to you this day in the city of David a Savior, who is Christ the Lord" (Luke 2:10–11). NKJV)

The whole company of angels began worshipping God and saying, "Glory to God in the highest. And on earth peace, goodwill toward men" (Luke 2:14 NKJV).

What a wonderful introduction to such a message of great joy with a promise of peace and goodwill!

For the longest time, I assumed this meant that people would live in peace and be kind to one another, especially at Christmastime when we tend to make a special effort to show goodwill toward those around us.

I believe that this "peace" and "goodwill" that God brought to us was not a reference to our attitudes toward one another; nor was it speaking of the end of wars and conflicts, for we can see that this has not yet happened, and wars and disharmony continue. It wasn't even referring to the amazing quietude of conscience that is ours at the new birth, although this is certainly a part of it.

This is speaking of the restoration of a relationship, the reconciliation of man brought back into fellowship with God, the possibility that we and our Maker would no longer be at odds with each another. All our needs and greatest desires, our endless searching and striving, the secret longing of every heart—all would now be met in this restored relationship, for the goodwill of God could be exhibited toward us through the promised Messiah.

Since that day when Adam left the very source of his life and welfare, the consequence of this rift has been evident throughout history in this troubled and sick world.

In the Greek, the word pronounced *i-rah-nay* means "peace" and also "prosperity" and is taken from a root word that means "to join" or "to be set at one" ("Greek Dictionary of the New Testament," *Strong's Exhaustive Concordance of the Bible*).

The Hebrew equivalent of this word is *shalom*, which is taken from a root word that means "to be safe" and "to make amends." The Hebrew expounds a little further in the meaning of this word. It speaks not only of being safe, restored, and friendly (on good terms) but also of welfare, which refers directly to health, prosperity, and peace (Hebrew and Chaldee dictionaries, *Strong's Exhaustive Concordance of the Bible*).

In the Jewish culture, when someone was setting out on a trip or embarking on some endeavor, it was customary to say to them, "Shalom," in the same way that we might say, "Have a good trip" or "God be with you." Shalom meant "Have a safe and prosperous trip." This word is also used as a greeting or in wishing someone well.

Our restored relationship with God implies so much more than our legal standing or forgiveness and acceptance, as amazing and wonderful as they are. It also implies a position of fellowship and all the associated benefits of that restored state.

From the giving of the law, through judges, kings, and poets, until Luke's writing of this account, man was not at peace with God. The only interaction between humanity and God was through the intervention of the law and the sacrifices. People were able to experience a measure of peace with God on a superficial and temporary level when, through the blood of animal sacrifice, they could find forgiveness. Year after year, sacrifices continued to be offered until Christ came (Hebrews 10:1–4).

What made this announcement and its ramifications so profound was the fact that it came into the Jewish world at a time when their whole life was wrapped around the law.

The keeping of the law availed for them benefits and blessings—all the things that God had intended for mankind from the beginning. Disobedience and departure from the law separated them from the blessings and resulted in all kinds of destruction. As well, the sacrifices—the shedding of the blood of various animals—gave them acceptance with God, though it was limited and temporary.

Going back to Luke's day and the words of the angel's announcement in proclaiming the "good news of great joy," we see that it was for "all people." It was not limited to the Jewish nation, for it reached beyond the law to something far greater. The law was given with "a better hope" (Hebrews 7:19).

The angel continued his announcement, saying, "For there is born to you [the Jewish nation] this day, in the city of David, a Savior, who is Christ the Lord" (Luke 2:11).

Few people really understood the good news or were willing to accept the Messiah when He came, for they continued to seek righteousness through keeping the law (Romans 9:31–32). How significant and necessary for us, today, to realize that blessings and favor with God are not dependent upon our works.

CHAPTER 11

A New Covenant

"The days come," says the Lord, "that I will make a new covenant."
—Hebrews 8:8

Knowing that His time to suffer was near, Jesus had arranged to eat the Passover meal with His disciples. He took the bread, blessed it, broke it, and gave it to them, saying, "This is my body that is given for you." After the meal, he took the wine and gave thanks, and passing it to each of them, he said, "This is the blood of the new covenant ... which is shed for many" (paraphrased from Matthew 6:22; Mark 4:22–23; Luke 22:19–20).

It was the first week of the Passover feast, and many Jews—doing as they had done every April for two thousand years—were preparing for the long journey to Jerusalem to purify themselves once again by the offering of a lamb.

No doubt, they were remembering the first Passover when the blood of a lamb had been put around the doorframes of their houses so that the angel of death would pass over. It was through this intervention of the blood that they were freed from Egyptian bondage.

There are many things I could say concerning the Passover feast, based on both the Old and New Testaments, but I am focusing on the heart of the new covenant. Although the things I'm sharing in these few chapters may not be new to you, I'm laying a foundation upon which I can rest the principles that I will be talking about in later chapters.

This particular Passover, when Jesus gathered with his disciples, was very different from all the previous ones, for He Himself was the Lamb that was to be offered, once for all. Paul eloquently spoke of this when he called Jesus the "mediator of a new covenant" and said that it spoke of "better things than Abel."

Abel was the son who brought his father, Adam, a lamb out of his flocks, "for he was a shepherd" (Genesis 4:1–4). Cain, in contrast, offered his father the fruit of his own labors and efforts—or his own good works, you might say. In a sense, we can see in this an illustration of our presenting God with Jesus the Lamb, our substitute, instead of our efforts to keep the law.

Again, Paul expounded on the fact that Jesus, through his death, burial, and resurrection, had "obtained [for us] a more excellent ministry," as He was the "mediator of a new covenant ... established upon better promises" (Hebrews 8:6). Paul concluded by saying that, in presenting a "new covenant, He has made the first old." In the Greek, the word translated "old" implies being "decayed," "worn out," and "obsolete."

We know that this provision of salvation didn't demolish the law itself, for all God's principles are good and beneficial for us. It was the old *system*—the keeping of the law as a means for acceptance with God—that became obsolete. We are now considered righteous before God—in Christ, not by our works—for God had in mind a more excellent way.

All Christian understand that Jesus' death on the cross coincided with the feast of Passover. As Jesus took upon Himself our sins, and ultimately delivered us from death, he was the fulfillment of the Passover lamb.

In contrast few Christians realize the significance of the fact that the outpouring of the Holy Spirit coincided with the feast of Pentecost.

What is the connection between the giving of the Holy Spirit and Pentecost? Many of us have come to associate this word with the outpouring of the Holy Spirit, but the word *Pentecost* means fiftieth, in reference to the fiftieth day after Passover.

To understand what this means, we have to look back into the old testament, where this feast began.

In Lev. 23:5, we read that in the evening of the fourteenth day of the first month, the Israelites partook of the Passover meal before leaving Egypt. In Exod. 19:1 we see Israel arriving at the wilderness of Sinai, on the first day of the third month. Then in Exod.19:10&11, we're told that on the third day of the third month Moses went up into the mountain where he received the ten commandments from God.

Year after year the Jews continued to celebrate the feast of weeks, or as it was later called, the feast of Pentecost, marking the time from their deliverance from bondage to the giving of the laws.

So what is the connection between the law and the giving of the Holy Spirit?

A few thousand years before Jesus came, Jeremiah spoke this prophecy, right in the midst of Israel's sins as they stood on the brink of going into captivity. Inspired by the Holy Spirit, Jeremiah said, "Look, the days are coming, says the Lord, when I will put my laws in their inward parts, and write them in their hearts … and I will be their God and they shall be my people" (Jeremiah 31:33–34).

He continued, expounding on this new reality when he said, in essence, "It won't take great amounts of teachings or preaching, but all will know Him, from the least to the greatest." Finally, the opportunity for relationship with God on a personal level was possible for any and all who would come to Him. It is only through the intervention of His Spirit abiding in us, that we can know Him personally.

Jesus said, "When the Comforter is come, whom I will send on to you from the Father, the Spirit of Truth, which proceeds from the Father, he shall testify of me." Jn. 15:26. And in John 16:13, Jesus tells them, "when the Spirit of Truth is come, he will guide you into all truth."

In Gal. 5:22, Paul explains that the work of the Holy Spirit within our hearts will produce good character qualities in our lives, such as: love, peace, patience, and goodness." So that it will no longer be a matter of our trying to keep the law, and laboring to do the right thing.

Paul later quoted Jeremiah: "This is the covenant that I will make with them after those days, says the Lord: I will put My laws into their hearts, and in their minds I will write them." (Hebrews 10:16 NKJV).

After Jesus' resurrection, He came to the house where the disciples were hiding for fear of the Jewish leaders who were seeking their lives. When they recognized Jesus, He said to them, "As the Father has sent me, so I send you." Then he breathed on them and said, "Receive the Holy Spirit" (John 20:22). For He knew that without His help they couldn't do what He was commissioning them to do.

When we are first saved, the Holy Spirit comes to abide in us. It's here that He begins His work of convicting, comforting, guiding, and counseling us. This, I believe, is the means by which He is writing God's laws upon our hearts and in our minds, as we cooperate with Him.

Before Jesus was to return to the Father, He told his disciples to wait together for the completion of the promise of the Father (Acts 1:4–5). During the days of the feast of Pentecost, the disciples were waiting and praying when the power of the Holy Spirit came upon them.

It's true that the Holy Spirit had been given to them prior to the day of Pentecost—as it is with us when we first accept Christ. The Holy Spirit was already accomplishing in their hearts, the inner work that He had been sent to do. When the Holy Spirit came "upon them" in the upper room, they were empowered with spiritual gifts and inspiration. With the Spirit's enabling, they could give expression to God's transformation in their lives in far greater ways than they could have done by themselves or by their own resources. This empowering is also promised to us today.

So, what is it about the new covenant that differentiates it from the old? The old covenant was an *external* covenant because it focused on a structure of laws that rested on their works and performance. While the new covenant, on the other hand, is an *internal* covenant whereby His Spirit within our hearts transforms us, through a personal relationship, to delight to do His will.

CHAPTER 12

He Is Risen

"Why do you seek the living among the dead? He
is not here [in the tomb] but he is risen"
—Luke 24:5&6 NKJV

In order for us to walk in this new covenant, it's necessary that we understand what it is that has made it possible for us to do so.

Let me take you back, once again, to a time in Israel's history. It was the tenth day of the seventh month, and the people of Israel were waiting anxiously in the outer court of the tabernacle for the return of the high priest (Leviticus 23:26–32).

For seven days prior to this day, the high priest had been purifying himself for the Day of Atonement. Not only was the sacrifice to be completely pure, but it was paramount that the high priest himself not be defiled in any way.

He spent much time diligently rehearsing in his mind every aspect of the tasks he would have to perform that day. Any error would certainly result in his death, and the offering for the sins of the people would not be accepted.

Throughout the year, individuals would come to the outer court of the sanctuary, and the priest would offer for them on the brazen altar various sacrifices—for sins, cleansing, and thanksgiving. The Day of Atonement was different. On that day, only once a year, the high priest alone would enter the sanctuary and proceed past the veil into the Holy of Holies. There he would sprinkle the blood of the sacrificial lamb on and in front of the mercy seat.

The mercy seat was the covering on top of the ark of the covenant. Scripture tells us that in the tabernacle of Moses, God's presence remained over the ark and the tabernacle—as a cloud by day and fire by night—leading and protecting them (Joshua 3:3, 8). Later, in the time of the kings whenever Israel went into battle, they carried with them the ark of the covenant, for it represented and assured them of God's presence with them (1 Samuel 4:21, 30; 1 Chronicles 14:20). Similarly, when the high priest sprinkled the blood on and before the ark, it represented the sacrifice of the Lamb (Jesus), presented for our sake before God.

When the priest finally emerged from the tabernacle, the "jubilee trumpet" was sounded, and a great rejoicing broke out among the people. They knew then that their sacrifice had been accepted by God and their sins had been forgiven—in this case, covered for another year.

Like the high priest emerging from the sanctuary, the resurrected Jesus walked out of the tomb, having wrought a greater victory for us and fulfilling a long-awaited promise.

Our sins are forgiven, and now we have the great hope of heaven's eternal joy.

But is that really *it*? Is that *all* of it? For so many Christians, these words, though true and foundational to our faith, seem to encapsulate the totality of their hope. It's as if that was all that Jesus accomplished for us.

I can remember watching TV programs at Easter when I was a child. In those days, the truth of the Bible was accepted and acknowledged, even in Hollywood. Though I had no understanding of what Easter was all about, seeing the things that Jesus suffered left me with a sense of sadness. I used to cringe and almost close my eyes until the part where He rose from the dead. I didn't know what the story was all about, but I was relieved by the final scene.

It's difficult for us to fathom what Jesus suffered for us, but every aspect of his suffering and victory is a component of our redemption and full salvation—from the insults and accusations of the crowds to His being examined and scrutinized by the high priest and the governor, Pilate, who found no fault in him; from His suffering on the cross to his descent into hell, or Hades, the place or state of departed souls;[1] from His resurrection to His ascension to the right hand of God.

I have the impression that in many churches, even today, there seems to be a kind of mystery surrounding Easter, a cloudy perception of what, in fact, Jesus actually accomplished for us.

When I think of the high priest in the temple during Old Testament times, performing his duties at different times of the year, it all seems strange and hard to understand. I can't say that I fully understand all that Jesus did or how the priest's actions were a picture of Jesus's sacrifice, but I do know this: all that Jesus accomplished through his sufferings, death, burial, and resurrection was for us, and it represents so much more than most of us seem to realize.

Let's consider some of those things.

As Christians, we all know that Jesus took upon Himself our sins. In doing so, all of God's wrath and judgment came rushing upon Him (Romans 5:9; 1 Thessalonians 1:10). This is the punishment that you and I deserved, but He bore these things in our place so that we wouldn't have to. There will be a day of judgment, but how can we who are now in Christ be judged for our works when our acceptance with God is no longer dependent upon our works? (Romans 3:20, 22). I believe that we will be judged in accordance with what we did with Jesus and all that He accomplished for us. The issue must be whether or not we believe and trust in what Jesus has given us through his death, burial, and resurrection.

In reference to his upcoming suffering on the cross, Jesus said, "Now is the judgment of this world: now the ruler of this world will be cast out. And I, if I be lifted up from the earth, will draw all to Myself." (John 12:31–32). In the New King James Version, the word *men* is italicized, indicating that it was not in the original text but was added by the translators to read: "I will draw all men unto me."

It's true that when we "lift Him up" with our praise and testimony to the world, men and women may be drawn to Him, but this is not what this verse is referring to. Jesus was talking about the judgment of God on the sins of the world. It is apparent that as Jesus took our sins upon

---

[1] *Strong's Exhaustive Concordance*, from the original Greek and Hebrew. *Hell* is translated from the Greek word *Hades*, the place where the departed souls of the just rested. Before Jesus completed the work of salvation, they had no access to heaven.

Himself on the cross, he also bore the judgment thereof in our place. Jesus said, "As Moses lifted up the serpent in the wilderness, even so must the Son of man be lifted up [on the cross]" (John 3:14; Numbers 21:8–9) so that "whosoever believes on him should not perish but have eternal life" (John 3:16). When Moses lifted up the serpent on the pole, all those who looked upon it were healed of their disease and didn't die.

Regarding Jesus's words in John 12:31–32, John explained, "This he said, signifying what death he should die." Certainly Jesus's taking our sins in His death on the cross could only result in the judgment that those sins deserved, even though Jesus Himself had never sinned.

Many Christians still hold to the belief that when we sin, the Devil has a right to work in our lives. In his letter to the Colossians, Paul told us that Jesus defeated the Devil at the cross. Jesus himself said, in reference to the cross, that "the prince of this world" would be "cast out" (John 12:31–32), and certainly He meant what He said.

Paul said it this way: "Blotting out the handwriting of ordinances that was against us, which was contrary to us [speaking of the law that we couldn't keep], he took it out of the way, nailing it to his cross … and having spoiled principalities and powers, made a show of them openly, triumphing over them in it (Colossians 2:14–15). "In bearing our sins and taking for us the punishments required by the law, he nullified [destroyed] the devil's right to work in our lives" (1 John 3:8). It was through the law—and the principle of blessings for obedience and curses for disobedience—that the Devil had any right to castigate us.

Of course, we're all well aware of the fact that the Devil is our enemy. He continues to attempt to influence us with lies and temptations, to infiltrate our lives with troubles and sickness whenever he can. He is an opportunist and will try to take advantage of our weaknesses until the day of judgment (Jude v.6), even though he has no legal right to do so.

James clearly defined the issue when he reminded us that each of us must take personal responsibility not to give in to sin. "But every man is tempted, when he is drawn away of his own lust, and enticed. Then when lust has conceived, it brings forth sin: and sin, when it is finished, brings forth death" (James 1:14–15)KJV. Because of Jesus, the Devil does not have a legal right to do anything in our lives, and therefore, if we are in Christ, we have authority over the Devil (Luke 10:17–19; Matthew 28:18–19; Luke 16:15–18).

In considering what was accomplished for us, many of us tend to overlook the fact that, in taking our sins and the legal consequences, Jesus bore our sicknesses and diseases, which were a part of the curses (Deuteronomy 28:59–61). Isaiah clearly shared this reality in his prophecy about Jesus in a way that leaves no doubt.

In Isaiah 53:4–5, he wrote, "Surely, He has born our sicknesses." The Hebrew word for *sickness* is taken from a root word meaning "infirmity, to be rubbed or worn out." It is the word for "malady, anxiety, disease, and sickness" as well as "calamity and grief." Isaiah went on to say, "And [he] carried our affliction." The Hebrew meaning here is "to spoil"—as in robbing or carrying away spoils in a battle—and "anguish" or "to have pain." I dare say that these two verses refer specifically to Jesus's provision and God's desire for our physical and emotional healing and health.

Isaiah also said, "Yet we esteem him stricken, smitten by God, and afflicted." [All these words point to a physical experience.] "But he was wounded for our transgressions, he was bruised for our iniquities. The chastisement of our peace [the punishment he suffered to restore our peace] was upon him, and by his stripes we are healed." Isaiah 53:4&5

This, I feel, is a significant issue, because many Christians tend to think that healing is a little something extra (if they believe it at all). Since Jesus took our sickness and diseases upon Himself on the cross, we can know for certain that it is significant to God.

When Jesus hung on the cross, carrying our sins, it was the sixth hour, which would be around noon, and "there was darkness over the whole land until the ninth hour" (Mark 15:33). As Jesus, the "light in this world," bore our sins "in his own body" (1 Peter 2:24), I believe that His experience could only be expressed by three hours of darkness.

Dr. James B. Richards, author and pastor of Impact Ministries of Huntsville, Alabama, suggests that this darkness was a means of covering what no one could look upon. Isaiah described Jesus as one whose "visage was so marred more than any man" (Isaiah 52:14). He took upon Himself all the sins—the judgment and the curses as well as the sicknesses and diseases—of all humanity.

In the darkness of that day at the ninth hour (around 3:00 p.m.), Jesus cried, "My God, my God, why have You forsaken me?" (Mark 15:34). At that moment, bearing our sins, Jesus was alienated from God, separated from the sense of His presence.

This brings up an age-old question among Christians about the idea that Jesus was both God and man. I have purposely not included any references to that issue here, because my focus in this book is not to debate but to simply share what I—and many others I've mentioned—have come to believe. I have spoken with many people who hold to this view, and I must admit that there are no verses in the Bible that actually say that Jesus was both man and God while He was on earth.

In Mathew 15:34, it is clear that only a man could suffer thusly and feel forsaken of God. If Jesus was 100 percent God and 100 percent man while He was on earth, how could He actually have suffered and died? God cannot die. Jesus's temptations, sufferings, and death would then have had to be figurative or symbolic. Jesus emptied Himself of all His glory and power when He humbled Himself to come down to earth for the love of mankind (Philippians 2:5–7; 2 Corinthians 8:9). He showed us what a man could do when he was uncompromisingly yielded to and fully dependent upon God. Jesus said, "I can of my own self do nothing" (John 5:19, 30). He taught us that we too are to rely upon and abide in Him (John 15:5).

Then He said, "It is finished" (John 19:30). And, as though he had regained his focus on God and remembered His love, He cried in a loud voice: "Father [not *my God* but *Father*], into Your hands I commend [entrust] my spirit [and soul]."[2] At that point, the veil of the temple was torn from top to bottom. Jesus's alienation from the Father by our sins now availed us of access to and acceptance by God.

When Jesus said "it is finished," He wasn't just referring to the completion of His earthly ministry and mandate, although that certainly was the case. It was also a declaration of the culmination of God's intention for mankind since the beginning. Every type and shadow in the Old Testament pointed to Jesus and God's intent and provision for us: the prophecy after the fall, which spoke of the seed of the woman crushing the head of the Serpent (Genesis 3:15); the sacrifices and feasts; all the promises in scripture; and the blessings offered under the law and spoken of in the Psalms and the Prophets.

But His complete victory for us was not entirely finished. The "jubilee trumpet," so to speak, had not yet sounded. Carrying our

---

2   The Greek word *pnyoo-mah* (G4151 and G4154) means "current of air," "spirit," and also "(human) rational soul" (*Strong's Concordance*, original Greek).

sins, Jesus died and descended into hell, or Hades (the place or state of departed souls).

To understand this, we can look back to a question put to Jesus by some of the scribes and Pharisees: "Teacher, we want to see a sign from you." (Matthew 12:38–39 NKJV).

"Show us a sign" was a request they often made. Many times they demanded a further miracle or some great act to prove who He was. Even while He was on the cross, the chief priests said to Him, "Come down from the cross that we may see and believe" (Mark 15:32).

But this time He said to the scribes and Pharisees, "An adulterous generation seeks after a sign … No sign will be given to it except the sign of the prophet Jonah. For as Jonah was three days and three nights in the belly of the great fish, so will the Son of Man be three days and three nights in the heart of the earth" (Matthew 12:39–40; Jonah 2:1–9 NKJV).

We read about Jonah's cry in the belly of the fish, and in it we see, as it were, a prophecy and a picture of Jesus. In the depths of hell, separated from His loving connection with the Father, He was, as Jonah said, "cast out of your sight; yet I will look again towards Your holy temple" (Jonah 2:4). Jesus was held in death by our sins, but he refused to regard "lying vanities" (Jonah 2:7–9 KJV; Acts 2:25–28; Psalm 16:7–10). Instead He turned His focus on God and His Word and promises.

Yes, I believe that Jesus, as a man, was full of the grace of God, and that through faith He overcame and conquered our sin, death, and the grave. We witness this when we read that He was tempted of the Devil in the wilderness but that He put His trust in God's Word (Matthew 4:1–11); or when He held five loaves and two fish and looked to God for the solution rather than looking at the problem (Matthew 14:15–21).

I believe it was through the exercise of His faith and trust in the Father that Jesus—as a man in fellowship with and full of God—overcame for us, was raised from the dead, and is now seated at the right hand of God, having a name above all names. And at the name of Jesus, every knee shall bow (Philippians 2:10).

CHAPTER 13

Salvation: The Eternal Now

"Now my eyes have seen your salvation."
—Luke 2:30

So amazing and so incredible is God's love for us, which was demonstrated through Jesus! The full extent of what was accomplished for us through His death, burial, and resurrection is so much more than we realize.

As we read the scriptures and consider the many prophesies[3] and promises[4] spoken or alluded to, we see that God's will and purposes for us have always been good, with the intent to restore, redeem, heal, and prosper us, not just morally but in every way. Before the very foundation of the world,[5] the intention of God's heart toward mankind was his full salvation, and that through Jesus.[6]

As my understanding of the scriptures, especially concerning this great salvation, has grown through the years, I have become aware of the fact that many Christians seem to hold to a limited view of what this salvation actually means in our lives.

When we hear the word *salvation*, we generally think of the "new birth," evangelism, and our hope for heaven. These things, of course,

---

[3]   Ezekiel 22:29–30; Isaiah 59:16, 20.

[4]   Jeremiah 30:17; Psalm 35:27.

[5]   Ephesians 1:4–5; Revelation 13:8.

[6]   Genesis 3:15.

are a true and real part of salvation, but by no means do they present the whole picture.

Let's looking at Luke's account[7] of the angel declaring the fulfillment of the promise that had been prophesied through Isaiah many years earlier. The angel said, "Unto you is born this day, in the city of David ... a Savior, Christ the Lord."

Here the Greek word *so-tare* is translated "savior" or "deliverer" and comes from a root word meaning "to be safe, delivered, or protected." It also means "to heal and make whole" and "cause to do well."[8]

The word translated as "savior," taken from the Hebrew word *yesh-oo-aw*, presents a similar thought. It speaks of something "saved" as well as "gaining victory" and "prosperity." This Hebrew word comes from a root word that means "to be open wide" or "free" (in the sense of having no worries or concerns, or "free as a bird"). It also speaks of being "helped" and "defended" and "getting the victory"[9]. It certainly sounds to me like something more than just being morally saved from our sins—although, praise God, that's a real part of it.

In the Old Testament times, when the Jewish people read the scriptures[10] or heard the prophecies[11] and considered the promise of "salvation" or the coming "Savior," they didn't perceive it as we do today. When they looked forward to the coming Messiah, they were not thinking in terms of forgiveness and hope for heaven as we do, although the annual sacrifices did speak to the sin issue.

But much of their hope and longing was set on such things as deliverance[12] and restoration from bondage, slavery, and political oppression,[13] as well as freedom from poverty and lack,[14] all of which were curses written in the law. Having memorized scriptures from childhood, the Jews were very familiar with the promises and blessings

---

[7]   Luke 2:10–11.

[8]   Dictionary of original Hebrew and Greek words, *Strong's Exhaustive Concordance of the Bible.*

[9]   *Strong's Concordance.*

[10]   Psalm 20:5.

[11]   Exodus 6:5; John 2:25; Isaiah 14:3.

[12]   Psalm 14:7; Isaiah 19:20.

[13]   Isaiah 9:6–7.

[14]   Deuteronomy 15:6.

typified in the Year of Jubilee.[15] Even their Hebrew customs and traditions (feasts days and sacrifices) solidified their confidence in God's goodwill and promises. But in all this, they didn't understand what this salvation really meant.

It's no wonder that when Jesus came, the Jews expected Him to set up a literal kingdom and to rule from the throne of David and restore the nation of Israel to power and blessing.

The Pharisees demanded that Jesus tell them when the kingdom of God was to come. He said, "The kingdom of God comes not with observation."[16] The original language makes it clear that the kingdom doesn't come by our "inspection, observation, or ocular evidence."[17]

Jesus concluded with a strange comment (to their way of thinking) when he said, "The kingdom of God is within you," speaking of God's rule and lordship in our hearts.

Jesus taught many things about the kingdom of God through parables and illustrations. He said that those who put their trust in earthly wealth will find it hard to enter the kingdom.[18] This internal kingdom rule requires our trust in God and His provision. Jesus said, "Seek first the kingdom of God and His righteousness, and all these things [that we need or seek after] will be added to you."[19]

The kingdom of God is like a treasure hidden in a field, and a person would be willing to sell all that he has in order to possess that field, so valuable and precious is this kingdom.

Jesus told the disciples that we have to be ruthless and unwavering in our pursuit of this kingdom, ridding ourselves of anything that would distract or divert our hearts.[20] It is far better to do without than to forfeit this kingdom, but in doing so, we find that His provision supplies abundantly beyond anything that we can give up. As well, Jesus explained that we must receive this kingdom as children, in simple trust.[21]

---

[15]   Deuteronomy 15:1–3; Obadiah 1:17.

[16]   Luke 17:20–21.

[17]   Greek dictionary, *Strong's Exhaustive Concordance*.

[18]   Matthew 19:24; Luke 10:24.

[19]   Matthew 6:33; Luke 12:31.

[20]   Mark 9:47; 12:34.

[21]   Matthew 10:14–15.

We see in Jesus's ministry that the kingdom of God took priority. It wasn't so much to bring us to repentance from sin but to restore us to relationship with God and to establish his kingdom within our hearts).

At one point, Jesus said, "I must preach the kingdom of God in other cities; for this reason am I sent."[22] Luke told us that Jesus went through every city and village with the twelve disciples, preaching and sharing the good news of the kingdom of God."[23] He instructed them to "heal the sick" and to say, "The Kingdom of God is come near to you."

He demonstrated the kingdom by saying, "If I, with the finger of God, cast out devils, no doubt the Kingdom of God is upon you."[24] In this way, the kingdom of God was made evident in a man. I believe that this internal lordship is reflected in this great salvation and should be evident in our lives.

It's clear to me that this internal lordship—the Holy Spirit working in our hearts and affecting our thoughts and motives—*must* be made evident in our lives.[25] We can also experience, on a daily basis, all the benefits of this great salvation that Jesus wrought for us. We should expect to see such things as healings (physical and emotional) and deliverance[26] from the oppression of disease, depression, fear, and so on. He will lead us to the point where we will have victory through the problems we face in this life, and we can prosper in the things we do[27] as effectual witnesses of the kingdom.

These things cannot be meant only for heaven, because it's here in this troubled world that we need them.

"In his book, *Divine Conspiracy*, Dallas Willard argues that the gospel preached in most evangelical churches today amounts to sin management and behavior modification.[28] He says, "Does Jesus only allow me to make the cut when I die? It's good to know that when I die, all will be well, but is there any good news for life [here and now]? If I

---

22 Luke 4:43.

23 Luke 8:1.

24 Luke 11:20.

25 2 Corinthians 2:14.

26 Colossians 1:12–13.

27 Romans 5:17.

28 Taken from Grant Thorp's blog, *Perspective Online*, 2012.

had a choice, I would rather have a car that runs than good insurance on one that doesn't."

It seems to me that we Christians have a limited and linear perspective of God, His will, and His ways. We seem to think that our salvation had a beginning and that it started when we accepted Jesus as Savior and Lord. Although, in a sense, that's when it begins for the individual, the truth is that the moment we received Him, we entered (accessed, or came in tune with) the eternal realm. Because we live in the realm of time, it is difficult for us to conceive of anything outside of time.

In the same way, we look to the future (and heaven) for the benefits of our salvation to begin, but even this is not entirely the case. The fact is that the moment we received Jesus, we actually stepped into a realm, or reality, that has always existed. It's the eternal "now," which has no beginning or end. By walking in faith in view of this salvation, we learn to access these things, which are already ours in Christ because of His finished work.

For forty days after Jesus's resurrection, He spoke to His disciples of the "things pertaining to the Kingdom of God."[29] (Wouldn't you love to have been there, listening and learning all those things pertaining to the kingdom? I certainly would. Of course, today we have the Holy Spirit to teach us about these things.

Jesus continued, "You shall receive power when the Holy Spirit is come upon you: and you shall be witnesses unto me, both in Jerusalem, and in Judea, and in Samaria, and to the ends of the earth."

Israel understood the external benefits of this promised salvation, but they didn't recognize the Savior when He came, and they couldn't conceive of an internal rule. All Christians recognize the promises of salvation as fulfilled in heaven, and many see the significance of God's internal kingdom in their hearts, but very few, it seems, realize the effects and benefits of this salvation for here and now where we need it the most.

Life can be challenging at times. While we are in this world, we will encounter physical, emotional, relational, and even financial problems. In the fellowship church, I saw people come in with problems and go out with the same problems—and maybe more. It troubled me that no one really found much help. I saw couples at odds with one another for

---

[29]   Acts 1:3.

years, and they never really resolved those issues or took hold of the internal help that was available to them—and to us all—in Christ.

I struggled with self-worth issues for years, reading self-help books and speaking with pastors, without finding the help I needed—until I realized His love and internal present help. In the fellowship church, we spent many hours praying for the sick while we watched some of them slowly die. Many considered these things a normal part of our lives, and some even assumed that it was God's will, never realizing the wonderful provision that Jesus wrought for us.

Many churches have dedicated, anointed pastors who preach Holy-Spirit-inspired messages, and many of these churches have counseling courses and cell groups. But we often seem to miss the practical aspects of salvation—peace, prosperity, healing, deliverance, and victory—putting them off until heaven.

Jesus's provision is sufficient and available to us now through an internal (heart) relationship with Him.

It's humbling to think that so great a salvation is offered to us and that by faith we can experience its benefits in our lives here and now.

If these things are true—and they are—what is hindering us from experiencing it?

CHAPTER 14

Mixing the Covenants

"If you don't stay on course you won't reach your goal"
-Author unknown

If we don't recognize the goodwill of God toward us, as demonstrated throughout the Bible, and if we don't accurately understand the fullness of what Jesus has availed for us, how can we possibly have the faith to take hold of these things?

There is a dangerous and destructive thinking among Christians that is inconsistent with Jesus's teachings, example, and provision. I saw this in the fellowship and have seen it in many churches since then. It lingers in the hearts and minds of sincere Christians, and I have seen it in my own thinking at times.

It's an insidious, faith-destroying hindrance to Christian maturity and stability, and it dilutes our testimony. It keeps us from fully trusting in and experiencing God's love and the benefits of walking with Him in this life. It causes us to wander in the foggy no-man's-land of uncertainty and confusion. It is a perspective that makes much of God's Word seem complicated, contradictory, and hard to understand.

The culprit is this: mixing the covenants.

As I mentioned in chapter 11, the old covenant that God made with Israel involved the keeping of the laws and sacrifices as a means of access to and acceptance with God. Their obedience availed for them all His blessings in the form of healthy, peaceful lives.

The new covenant, by contrast, is not about our ability to keep the laws or change our behavior. It's about having a new, transformed heart. Through Jesus's death, burial, and resurrection, we are "made nigh to God" in a unique relationship whereby we can, through faith, access all the resulting benefits.

We all know, to some degree, that Jesus has brought us into a new covenant with God, but for the most part, there seems to be some confusion about what it really means to leave behind the old covenant and move forward into the new. Many times, unknowingly, we drift back and forth between the two covenants. We acknowledge the principles of the new covenant, or we can at least verbalize terminologies such as *faith, righteousness, grace,* and *relationship.* The problem is that we try to apply these principles with an old-covenant perspective, and if we are looking for more than empty religion or behavior modification, it just doesn't work.

For instance, when we try to operate faith by trusting God for healing, we look to the old covenant and wonder if He's willing to do it this time. We may be seeking fellowship with God, but then we stumble over our shortcomings, and in self-condemnation, we distance ourselves from Him.

When I came to realize some erroneous beliefs within the fellowship, I searched for clarity of understanding. I began to read and listen to many different ministers, whom I mentioned earlier: believers from the 1600s to the present day. Many of them had a profound effect on my thinking and my faith. They were people like John G. Lake, F. F. Bosworth, Kenneth and Gloria Copeland, James B. Richards, and others who dared to believe all of God's Word and put it into practice in their personal lives and step beyond their own limitations. They found the capacity to experience healing and to exercise the authority that is ours in Christ. I then began to realize that these were not a special, anointed few. We too can live in this new covenant through the transforming power of the indwelling presence of the Holy Spirit.

During this time of searching, I came to realize that we must accurately recognize the difference between the two covenants. Otherwise, it's challenging to reconcile the God of the Old Testament with the God of the New Testament. One might think that He sometimes is full of compassion and reaches out to help and heal, while at other times He changes His mind and is silent and ready to punish us for our sins. First, we must be established in the fact of His unchanging character, integrity, and unconditional love. The fact is, the covenant changed, but God didn't.

Under the old covenant, God had to deal with man through laws and rules, and He could only speak to them externally through specially anointed prophets and signs, until Jesus came and dealt with the sin issue. In this new covenant, we are righteous before God, and that righteousness is not dependent upon our good works but rests on the fact that we are in Christ.

This fact is a vital part of the new covenant. Paul explained to the church in Corinth, "As in Adam all die, even so in Christ shall all be made alive.[30]" Being descended from Adam, we carried the sin potential and all of its consequences, which produced death in us. But now, with the new birth, we enter into a whole new position and identity "in Christ."

I believe that this phrase, used so many times in the epistles, is in reference to Jesus's words to His disciples[31] and all believers[32] when He said, "I am the Vine and you are the branches." In Romans 15:5, Paul said that we are one, sound whole in Christ. In 1 Corinthians 1:2, he told us that we are sanctified in Christ. In Galatians 2:4, he spoke of the liberty that is ours in Christ. Paul also spoke of being "found in Him, not having my own righteousness but the righteousness which is from God by faith."[33]

The idea that righteousness could be a free gift was beyond comprehension. This far-reaching idea is, in fact, the source of both incredible persecution by those who did not believe, and inconceivable power for those who did believe.[34]

James Richards wrote, "The sense of wholeness that comes through faith's righteousness breaks the crippling grip of religion and sets a person free to know the living God. It was not the idea that Jesus was Savior that made [Paul's writings] so radical. Many people who persecuted Paul believed that Jesus was Savior. The thing that was so

---

[30] 1 Corinthians 15:22

[31] John 15:5; 17:21–23.

[32] John 17:20.

[33] Philippians 3:9.

[34] Romans 1:16.

radical was the inconceivable idea that Jesus was our righteousness. This idea, which is the very core of the Gospel, has always been more than the natural man could grasp. Paul identified this belief as the stumbling stone of the Gospel, yet, amazingly, it is the heart of the gospel."[35]

Sometimes we look into the Old Testament for direction for our lives today, but the fact is that Jesus had not yet come, and people at that time didn't yet have the Holy Spirit within, as we do now, to teach them personally. As well, many of the things that Jesus showed us about God had not yet been revealed to them under the old covenant.

Although we can learn through their examples, be encouraged by God's faithfulness in their lives, and learn through the laws and principles, we cannot base our doctrine on old covenant standards. In order for us to understand and benefit from the Old Testament, we must read it from the perspective of the new covenant. Otherwise we will soon forget what Christ has done for us.

If, when you encounter difficulties in your life, you allude to Old Testament examples or, worse, refer to or quote Job, you are mixing the covenants. If you face a serious illness or tragedy and you ask "what did I do wrong?" or "why is God doing this to me?," you are confusing the two covenants. We must know with confidence what Jesus has wrought for us on the cross and through His resurrection. As well, we have to recognize that God will never violate what Jesus has done for us. In view of this, we can always know that He will never send sickness or trouble to punish or teach us anything.

Paul was exasperated when he heard that Peter, after telling the people that they didn't have to follow the Jewish laws in order to be right with God, then obligated them to be circumcised.[36]

Paul called the Galatians foolish, and he marveled that they so easily turned back to trusting the works of the law.[37] He went on to say that "no one is justified before God by keeping the law."[38] "I do not frustrate the grace of God," Paul continued, "for if righteousness comes by the law, then Christ is dead in vain."[39]

---

[35] James B. Richards, *Breaking the Cycle.*

[36] Galatians 2:14.

[37] Galatians 1:6–12.

[38] Galatians 2:16.

[39] Galatians 2:21; Romans 10:3–4.

Paul was accused of liberalism when he preached the truth about God's grace. Even today, many Christians believe that we are saved by God's grace but that we have to keep the law to be righteous. They argue that if we don't emphasize the law, then people will get into sin. We think we need to be constantly reminded of the law in order to keep us on track. We forget that through Jesus, God put His laws into our hearts. Now we have an awakened conscience, and if we are willing, with God's help we can live a righteous life. People will sin anyway, whether we bombard them with the law or not, if they are so inclined. Instead of memorizing the laws, maybe we should fix our attention on learning to be more sensitive to the Holy Spirit.

I have seen some Christians actually treating Jesus's teachings as though they were simply more laws for us to obey, and in this I believe they're missing the whole point of the new covenant. I'm not advocating throwing out the law; all scripture, when understood and used scripturally, is beneficial. But the new covenant is not about keeping external rules. It's about a relationship.

CHAPTER 15

Trials, Tests, and Tribulations

"Life is fraught with trouble and difficulties.
—Author unknown

Job said it this way: "Man is born unto trouble, as sparks fly upward."[40]

Equally so, life can be filled with very good things. There have been times in my life when I have felt extremely blessed. As I looked around, I could see answered prayers and promises fulfilled: good health, a great relationship, and a beautiful home in a peaceful place. Other times I have felt as though I was under a curse.

At one point I was experiencing some health concerns, and on top of that, I was not sleeping well. I was unable to write and was consequently delaying the completion of a book I was working on. My husband had to go away for a month at a time for work, and my job as an ESL tutor became redundant because there were not enough students to merit an assistant at that time. Nothing seemed to be going right. Fortunately, I didn't blame God. Instead I began to remind myself of His goodness and faithfulness, and shortly thereafter, things began to change for the better.

I've heard people say things like, "Trouble and hardship in this life are given so that we will long for heaven."

---

[40] Job 5:7.

How foolish to think this way, as if God had to make our lives so miserable that we'd say, "Anything would be better than this!" Such thinking would cause me to suspect that heaven may not be much better.

If God sends pain and suffering to us, why would (or how could) we then believe that heaven would be good and pleasant? Why wouldn't we then assume that heaven too must be fraught with troubles and pain in order to continue to keep us humble, even there. On the contrary, God wants us to see and know how loving, generous, and good He is so that we can then long to know Him more and anticipate a heaven filled with only good.

I have noticed, and I'm sure you have too, that both believers and nonbelievers alike experience both good and evil. Then we foolishly ask, "Why do bad things happen to good people?," as if being good merits us good things, and being bad earns evil things. This is not the new covenant. People who ask questions like this are living either under the old covenant or a mixture of the old and new. They have forgotten what Jesus has done for us, or they don't really know God's love. Because of Jesus's finished work, the new covenant is not about what we deserve.

Christians who are confused about the covenants tend to think that God blesses us sometimes but other times sees fit to curse us. In particular, when something bad happens, we assume that God sent it or allowed it. Oftentimes we assume that He orchestrates these things to teach us something or to produce some character trait in us. When we can't figure out the reason, we assume that it must have been sent with a purpose that is beyond our capacity to understand. For many years I assumed this was the case.

I used to believe that God uses difficulties to deal with our sinful nature. I was once part of a church that believed that God sends troubles—and even sickness and tragedy—to purge and purify us and make us acceptable to Him. We believed that every area of our lives had to be searched out and scrutinized by God in this way in order to build Christian character and bring us to maturity.

First of all, God is not interested in cleaning up our old nature with its flaws and failures. According to the apostle Paul, "The 'old person' is dead,"[41] and in Christ we must recognize and accept this reality. To the church in Rome, Paul said that we must "put off the old man" by disassociating ourselves with it. In his letter to the Corinthians, Paul

---

[41]   Romans 6:6.

told them, "If you are in Christ, you are now a new creation." We must live in view of this.

I often hear Christians quoting phrases from scripture such as "the refining pot for silver and the furnace for gold"[42] in reference to God's trials in our lives. We overlook the fact that Zechariah goes on to say, "But God tries the hearts." God's method of "dealing" with us is through searching and convicting our hearts, not sending hard circumstances and trials. The Holy Spirit is given to convict us from within our hearts, and no longer do we, like Israel of old, have to be afflicted with disease or dragged off into captivity by our enemies to cause us to repent.

Sometimes I wonder why it is that we don't seem to be able to simply accept God's love and goodwill for us as shown us through Jesus. It's as if we *want* to suffer, as if we feel the need to work for, or in some way merit, His blessings. We cannot fathom or even accept the fact that they are free because of Jesus.

Whenever the subject of God's dealing with people comes up, inevitably someone will mention Job or will quote the scripture that speaks of the "forty years that God humbled and proved Israel in the wilderness." Both Job and Moses, in a sense, lived under an old covenant mentality, for Jesus had not yet come. Job was, in fact, an example of a man living under the law and in fear, fluctuating between pride and condemnation—something we all tend to do when we live under such a mind-set.

A close friend and precious brother in the Lord had gone through a very difficult experience. His wife had been diagnosed with cancer, and as time went on, her health had declined to the point of being on life support. She continued in this state for almost a year, and during this time he had an affair with another woman. A short time later, he was confronted by someone regarding his actions. He described the confrontation: "God hit me with a two-by-four." He had told us previously that he felt as though God had left him, but now he felt that God was once again with him and working in his life.

I don't for a minute believe that God brought the cancer to teach him anything, and I know that God never left him, for He has promised never to leave or forsake us. Perhaps it was my friend who left God.

---

[42]   Zechariah 17:3.

Two-by-fours are not God's method of dealing with us, getting our attention, or keeping us on track. I've heard similar accounts by different people, but as Solomon said, "The rod is for the fool." If we are in Christ, we are not fools, though we may sometimes act that way. God doesn't whip us into line through difficult circumstances.

The big issue that comes up when we talk about the challenges of life is the "sovereignty of God." God is sovereign, so we assume that He can do whatever He chooses to do. Therefore, we conclude that whatever happens must be God's will.

No! There are some things that God will not—and I dare say, cannot—do. He will not do anything that would contradict what Jesus has done for us.

When Jesus came and hung on the cross, bearing our sins, He took the punishment that we deserved and should have suffered. The curse,[43] judgment,[44] and wrath of God came upon Him, but He bore it all in our place so that we wouldn't have to. It would be inconceivable now for us to assume that God would refute or reject what Jesus did for us, by punishing us when we fall short. If He was to send a curse—or anything included in the list of curses recorded in Deuteronomy—upon us when we sin, it would be as if God had decided that Jesus, in taking the curse in our place, had not been enough, and we must continue to bear the curse ourselves.

Difficulties will come in this world, Jesus told us. He said, "You will experience tribulation [temptations and adversity]."[45] He continued and added, "But be of good cheer [happy and courageous], for I have overcome the world." The word *overcome* means "to get the victory over, and to conquer." He has conquered the world and its influence and effect over us. In Him we can always have the victory, for He purchased it for us on the cross. Even through difficult times and adversity, we can, through faith in Him and His finished work, take hold of that victory.

Job said (and many Christians quote him today), "The Lord gives and the Lord takes away." Job again spoke out of his misconception of God and His intent, for the Messiah had not yet come. Jesus told us that "it is the thief that comes to steal and to kill and to destroy," not

---

[43]   Galatians 3:13.

[44]   John 12:32.

[45]   John 16:33.

God. He also said, "I am come that they might have life, and that they might have it more abundantly."

Yes, we will encounter various difficulties in this life.[46] Through these experiences, we have the opportunity to exercise the measure of faith we have been given so that it can grow stronger, and we can learn to patiently endure without wavering, holding to His Word by believing and trusting in His provision through Jesus. Through these situations in our lives, we can ask God for wisdom, trusting that He will give it to us.[47] As we listen and are willing to follow His direction, He will always lead us out of our troubles into victory—the victory Jesus already wrought for us.

I've heard too many messages from the pulpit using James's words to solidify a skewed, unscriptural perspective of temptation being God's vehicle for purification. James also exhorted us to "let no man say, when he is tempted, that he is tested of God." Then he said that God doesn't tempt anyone. The fact is, if we are tempted and succumb to it, we have to take personal responsibility and not blame God.[48] James exhorted us not to get this principle wrong, for all good things come from God, and He doesn't change His mind in this regard.[49]

Paul encouraged us to "glory in our tribulations."[50] Contrary to what many of us have been taught, we are to glory—and in this case, boast and give thanks—not for the hard situations that we assume will make us better people, but because we can always anticipate His help and victory[51] in any situation.

We don't passively become better people by going through hard times. I've seen people rally together during difficulties, selflessly helping one another. I remember at River Source Fellowship that there was a fire in the large log building we called the tabernacle, and it burned to the ground. At the time, people put aside their personal concerns and ran into the building to retrieve various items that were valuable to us—canned goods, milking equipment, some dishes, and even a piano.

---

46 James 1:2.

47 James 1:3–6.

48 James 1:13–15.

49 James 1:16–17.

50 Romans 5:3.

51 2 Corinthians 2:14.

Someone made sandwiches and tea and opened up her home, a humble log cabin, to feed everyone. Oddly though, a short time afterward, when things had returned to a state of normality, the very same people were again at odds with one another, fighting and arguing. Nothing had changed. We can grow through an experience only when we draw close to God and lean on Him. It's not the trial but a heart willing to trust God through it all that changes us.

In Peter's writings, he spoke of "the fiery trial which is to try you."[52] Again, this is not talking about God's "dealings" with us. In the Greek, the phrase *fiery trial* speaks of "calamity" and "conflagration" (a great, destructive fire). The word translated as "try" is taken from a root word that means "to scrutinize, entice, examine, prove, or tempt." We know by His Word that God does not put on us calamity or destruction; nor does He entice or tempt us. The Greek word for *try* speaks of "solicitation, provocation, and temptation."

It is clear that Peter was not referring here to something put upon us by God. In fact, the context seems to imply that what he calls "fiery trials" are actually persecution, for, after speaking of these "trials," he encouraged us to "rejoice, in as much as you are partaking of Christ's sufferings." As Jesus was harassed, spat upon, and even tempted and mocked, so in persecution many believers have suffered such things. Peter went on to say, "If you are reproached for the name of Christ, happy are you."

Although these painful trials are not God's will for us, many in the midst of persecution have chosen to draw near to God and have found His help. Amazingly, the church—that is, all believers in Christ—has grown in such times. It is not the persecution itself that accomplished anything but the fact that they put their trust in God.

We must be willing to suffer, if need be, for the furtherance of the gospel, but we can always know that God's will for us is good continually.

"Every challenge is an opportunity."[53] We are not victims in this life. Regardless of difficulties, we can, because of Jesus, be victors.

---

[52] 1 Peter 4:12–14.

[53] Quote by Conrad Black, author, investor, and former newspaper publisher who, for some years, controlled Hollinger International, the newspaper empire.

CHAPTER 16

What Is Grace?

"By faith we have access unto this grace wherein we stand,
and rejoice in the hope of the glory of God."
—Romans 5:2

The word *grace* is one of the most misunderstood and misused words in the New Testament. We confuse grace with mercy, and out of this misconception come all kinds of strange doctrines.

In Paul's letter to the Hebrews, it is clear that mercy and grace are not the same. He wrote, "Let us therefore come boldly unto the throne of grace, that we may obtain [both] mercy and grace to help in time of need." Clearly these words are not one and the same.

Since we are not under the law, some conclude that God's unmerited kindness (mercy) allows us to do whatever we please and to have whatever we want, with no responsibility or consequences. No wonder so many Christians (and pastors) tense up when they hear the term "the grace message." This is not what grace is about.

This has been a great controversy since the time of the early church. Some accused Paul of liberalism when he preached the message of God's grace.

"We are not under the law but under grace."[54] If we don't understand grace, this statement sounds like heresy.

I had heard all kinds of things about the "grace message" during my time spent in the Christian community, and none of it was good.

---

54   Rom. 6:14

When I read the Bible, I often wondered why Paul and other writers sometimes used the terms *grace* and *mercy* in the same sentence. If they meant the same thing, it would seem redundant to use the two words. None of the books I read helped to clarify the issue for me. It wasn't until years later, when I looked a little deeper into the original language, that I began to understand its meaning.

The word *grace* in the Greek is *charisiz*, from which we derive the word *charisma*. It is taken from a root word that means "kindness, cheerfulness, being calmly happy, and well off." It appears that these qualities are actually the effects of grace working in us.

The Greek word translated as "grace" speaks of divine influence upon or within the heart of the believer and its reflection in our lives. This Greek word also speaks of "enablement" and "capacity."

This influence is much more than the stirring upon our hearts at initial salvation, but I believe it is meant to be—as with everything we received at that time—an ongoing experience in our hearts, which has the potential, with our cooperation, to have an effect on our lives.

The best encapsulated definition I have heard that clearly distinguishes *mercy* from *grace* is this: "Mercy offers me forgiveness when I sin; while grace gives me the power to not sin."[55]

Grace is not, as we have believed, synonymous with mercy. It is something very different. With mercy, God is still with us and for us even when we sin, but His grace works in us, inspiring us to better things.

Paul, in his letter to the Hebrews, said, "Let us therefore come boldly unto the throne of grace, that we may obtain mercy [unmerited and unconditional love and acceptance] and find grace [enablement] in time of need."[56]

At one point in the life of the apostle Paul, he was struggling with a problem that he couldn't seem to get on top of. It troubled him greatly, and he called it a "thorn in the flesh."

There are many scriptures in the Old Testament that speak of thorns and thistles. In most of these scriptures, the term *thorn* is referring to "a persistent temptation," a "troubling dilemma," or a "frustrating

---

[55] James B. Richards from his book "Grace the Power to Change"

[56] Heb. 4:16

circumstance," and sometimes it also refers to a "source of mental anguish."

Some believe that Paul's thorn was a physical illness, but scripture doesn't bear this out. He suffered many things in the course of his life and ministry, having been beaten, whipped, and stoned on several different occasions, almost to the point of death. Yet every time it happened, God apparently healed, restored, and raised him up, for shortly thereafter, he returned and continued to preach the good news.[57]

"Paul himself understood and preached the gospel of Jesus Christ, which included His provision for healing, as well as repentance and forgiveness of sins. How then would he have succumbed to his injuries or sickness? To even imply that God would allow such a thing would be a denial of the good news and what Jesus has done for us."[58] Paul, in fact, laid hands on the sick as part of his ministry, and they recovered.

One popular belief among some Christians is the idea that Paul suffered from some type of eye disease. The fact is, he was blinded in his encounter with an angel at his conversion, but shortly after that, scripture tells us that his sight was restored, and there is no mention of any relapses.

In reference to that time, some have said that they would have been willing to pluck out their own eyes for him[59], give him the clothes off their backs, or give up their right hand. Such was their love for him.

Someone once commented that surely Paul did have a problem with his eyesight, based on his mention of writing with "so large a letter." Once I was writing a letter to my stepfather, who was having difficulty reading fine print. I was careful to write a little larger than I usually do. When he wrote back to me, his own writing was the same size as it had always been. It would have been a ridiculous and unnecessary effort for him to write in large letters. Why, then, in Paul's case, if he couldn't see well, would he attempt to write large letters? Most likely, Paul was referring to the number of pages in his letter.[60]

---

[57] Acts 11:22; 14:8-19; Acts 11:26; 21:27; 21:30-33; 27:26-44

[58] A. B. Simpson, *The Lord for the Body.*

[59] Galatians 4:15

[60] Galatians 6:11.

As a side thought, I believe it's possible that Paul's "thorn in the flesh," which he referred to as a "messenger of Satan," was some kind of mental anguish. Perhaps it was his great desire to minister the gospel to the Jews (his own people), when God had sent him to the Gentiles.

Whatever Paul's problem may have been, we know that he prayed earnestly about it—three times, in fact.

In our limited understanding of grace, we miss the beautiful account of Paul's experience, and we misinterpret God's answer. When God said to Paul, "My grace is sufficient for you,"[61] we assume (when we mix mercy with grace) that in the midst the difficulty, Paul found comfort in the realization of God's merciful kindness toward him—and that was supposed to be enough for him to continue to endure this thing.

This is often our perspective in the face of our difficulties, and we do find comfort in His presence, regardless of the situation. But thank God that He offers us much more than that. He inspires and enables us to come out of our problem. He did this in my own experience when I found the courage to leave a church that had drifted into error, or when I struggled with fear and learned to trust in God's love for me and to stand in His Word.

God also said to Paul, "For my strength is made perfect in weakness." He was saying, in essence, "My grace—the empowering, enabling influence working in you—is sufficient for you and your problem."

If we will, in our own situations, relinquish our opinions, worries, and striving and lean on His ability within us, we will always find His solution. Whether we're struggling financially and can't even pay the rent, going through a nasty divorce, or facing sickness, we can draw near to God, and He will draw near to us. This place of trust is where we experience His comfort and help. We find that He won't let us down.

Peter tells us, "Cast all your cares upon Him, for He cares for you"[62] and "He gives grace to the humble."[63] Like Paul, we must cast our concerns, our thorns, our irritations and worries on Him, no matter how many times we need to do so, until our hearts are at peace and trusting God. Yielding in this way to His enabling grace, we find wisdom beyond our own and direction when we don't know what to do.

---

[61] 2 Corinthians 12:9.

[62] 1 Peter 5:6–7.

[63] 1 Peter 5:5.

Interestingly, Paul then concluded, saying, "Most gladly therefore will I rather glory in my infirmities [feebleness, weakness, inabilities], that the power [Greek meaning: "force, miraculous power, strength, or ability"] of Christ may rest upon me."

Paul encountered all kinds of difficulties, but he didn't stay there. He found the power to overcome every time, and so can we.

I just finished reading an account of some persecuted Christians who escaped from their country by stowing away in a metal container in a ship heading for Canada.[64] In the daytime, it was unbearably hot, and at night, they were freezing. At one point, having used up the oxygen, they had to drill holes in the container wall and use drinking straws to breathe. Finally, their container was loaded into the bottom of a ship. Their meager supply of water had run out, and they had reached the point of resigning themselves to death. In the midst of it all, songs and scriptures came to their minds, and they were reminded of other times on this journey when God had provided in miraculous ways. Even while suffering in fear, doubt, and despair, there was something working within them, inspiring faith, restoring hope, and stirring them on with a strength beyond their own. This is the power of "grace."

"Sometimes, the hardest things are just lifting places into the grace of God,"[65] wrote Smith Wigglesworth, who left his job as a plumber to pursue what grew into a worldwide evangelistic and healing ministry in the early 1900s.

"God's grace always takes us beyond the limits of our power and ability, and ushers us into His realm of power and ability."[66]

Have you ever been in a situation where someone had a need and you weren't sure what to say or you didn't feel qualified or equipped to counsel them? Then, in the course of the conversation, you were amazed at what came out of your mouth (wisdom beyond your own), but you knew (though you might have liked to take the credit, or maybe you just brushed it off as coincidence) that it wasn't you who were so smart or full of insight. It was God's wisdom that came alive in your heart, and you spoke it. That's grace working in you.

---

[64] Simon Ivascu and Wesley Pop, from their book and testimony, *The Price of Freedom*.

[65] Smith Wigglesworth, *Apostle of Faith*

[66] James B. Richards.

Grace enables us to do what we, of ourselves, cannot do. In difficult situations, we can yield to His grace within us and lean on Him, and so let His grace empower us to overcome our problems. In the end, it's not about what we have done, great or small, but whether or not we have done it by His grace.

"God is able to make all grace abound to you, that you having all sufficiency, in all things may abound to every good work."[67]

---

[67]   2 Corinthians 9:8.

CHAPTER 17

Christian Nonbelievers

"But without faith it is impossible to please God."
—Hebrews 11:6

Does God really want us to be happy, empowered, and victorious in our situations?

Could it really be that our God wants us to be healthy, prosperous, and furnished to succeed in this life? He has put us here to do a job, after all.

Many Christians quote and believe a popular saying, though it's unscriptural: "God is more interested in our character than our comfort." Though we reason that difficulties build character, hardship and trouble cannot of themselves produce anything in us at all, good or bad. Only a heart willing to abide in Christ will bear the fruit of godly character.

When I began to realize God's love and goodwill for us, and understood that He never sends or allows trouble for our instruction or perfection, my whole paradigm of the Christian life began to change dramatically.

I remember many times of crying out to God, asking, begging, and striving to persuade Him to meet my needs. I thought it pleased Him for me to grovel and humble myself in this way. In my fear and confusion, I lived in uncertainty, never sure if He would see fit to help or hinder. In fact, His desire to help was such that He had already provided the vehicle for meeting all my needs before I even experienced any lack.

Jesus Himself wrought a full victory for you and me through His death, burial, and resurrection.

It was a great breakthrough when I finally realized the fact that everything is now based on Jesus's finished work.

The fact is, when I first began to hear the truth of God's goodwill and intent for us here on this earth, it seemed too good to be true. I wished it were so, but I didn't dare believe it or even consider its implications in my life as a believer. Religion had wrapped its tentacles around my heart until I couldn't see past my own "unworthiness."

But now, in this new covenant, I am without excuse. I don't have to be bound by my old sins, failures, and tendencies, and neither do I have to live my life in misery and lack. In Christ, I have all that I need for my welfare and benefit, as well as the capacity to live a righteous, godly life.[68]

In spite of the fact that from the beginning of time and throughout the ages the very theme of creation has been the love and the goodwill of God, religion has diverted our hearts from the truth. When Jesus came to earth, His very life, words, and deeds were a demonstration for us of what God is like, and yet we seem to have missed it. When He took upon Himself the judgment that we deserved and availed for us every promise and provision, we deemed it presumptuous to take it. So we ate the crumbs and chose the law and our own efforts and merit.

I realize that this message of God's love and provision has been misrepresented. Sadly, there have always been, and will continue to be, those who pervert truth in their ignorance of God and His wisdom, principles, and love. The truth still remains the truth, regardless of who misuses it.

It's sad to hear of this kind of error, but even worse is the fact that it has marred the faith of many Christians today. Consequently, they struggle through life, living a half-truth and never knowing the transforming, empowering provision that is available to them.

It seems to me that many Christians, because of this kind of thinking, live a mediocre and powerless but "safe" life in which they hold on to enough truth to maintain their ticket to heaven. But their experience here is one of little real joy and none of the power they could have.

---

[68] 2 Peter 1:3.

In our disbelief, we hold to an old covenant perspective. In order to prop up our religious perceptions (opinions), we inadvertently construe doctrines to fit our experience. We struggle with our failures, ongoing sickness, and lack, and because we don't see any change, we assume it must be God's will. Then we find scriptures to confirm our view. Our personal struggles and shortcomings are not the "fellowship of His sufferings." Jesus suffered by taking our punishment so that we wouldn't have to. One important aspect of the fellowship we now share with Him is His victory.

Some say, "Why should we only accept good from God and not evil?" It is true that we can draw near to God and find comfort in times of trouble, but God doesn't send evil.

I've heard all kinds of unscriptural ideas, some of which claim that the "bad" things come from God to teach us, and the good things come from the Devil to tempt us.

Sometimes we experience a subtle feeling of unbelief that we can't always identify, but it influences and molds our trust—or mistrust—in God.

All our limited perceptions and religious ideas aside, we still stand incredulous. His love, goodwill, and provision for us seem too extraordinary to be possible.

According to the *Gage Canadian Dictionary*, the word *incredulous* means "to doubt, not ready (or willing) to believe, skeptical and disposed to doubt."

Perhaps we are experiencing what Jesus called "hardness of heart." This doesn't mean we are evil or that we are deliberately resisting God. Years of listening to messages that give us only a partial gospel (as I did) cannot help but distort our perception of God and His will. The challenges of life can erode our initial faith. All of these things posed a challenge to my faith in God at different times in own experience.

Faith is what God wants and expects from us. Life's problems can wear away our faith and confidence in God, and if we are not established in the whole truth of the gospel, these things can form a callus over our hearts until we are no longer sensitive to the voice of God and the good news.

Maybe it's been years since your faith was uncomplicated and you trusted God and knew that all things are possible.

Are we incredulous? Or are we willing to believe?

CHAPTER 18

The Beautiful Fight of Faith

"There is a power of faith that draws to us what seems impossible.
—John G. Lake

Can you remember a time when you were praying, reading the Bible, or just thinking deeply about God's Word, and suddenly you realized that your perspective had changed and your heart was filled with a sense of confidence unlike the emotions or thoughts you'd carried before? Whatever the influencing factor, your faith was suddenly alive.

This is a feeling beyond our five senses. It's a kind of deep, inner knowing that lifts us above our circumstances and awakens our confidence so we can say, "I believe."

From my teen years into my twenties and thirties, I frequently experienced debilitating migraine headaches, often brought on by stress. Doctors will tell you that there is no cure for migraines.

When I was in my early thirties, I began reading the Bible and some books[69] on the subject of healing. It was also around this time that I was listening to a series of tapes[70] that dealt with the biblical principles of physical healing. One tape in particular that had a profound effect on me and my faith was the testimony of Dr. James B. Richards's own

---

[69] Books by John G. Lake and Smith Wigglesworth.

[70] *Supernatural Healing*, a CD series by Dr. James B. Richards. See impactministries.com/store.

experience with healing. After applying principles of faith over a period of time, he was healed of a congenital, life-threatening kidney disease.

One rather stressful morning at the River Source Fellowship, I was preparing a meal for the school, which I did once a week. I was also preparing for an art class I would be teaching that afternoon. Things in the kitchen were not going as smoothly as I would have liked, and the meal was going to be a little late. I began to experience the symptoms associated with the onset of a migraine, which included a sensation of flashing lights piercing through my line of vision.

Inspired by the tapes I had been listening to, I quickly excused myself—having finally gotten the meal to where it could be served—and found a quiet place to pray. I worshipped God for a short time in order to get my focus off the problem and on Him, my healer. This is not a formula, but I simply began confessing the truth of Jesus's provision: that He has taken and conquered all our sickness and diseases as well as our sins.

I had just been reading and thinking about Proverbs 4:20–23, where Solomon instructed us to put our attention on God's Word. In reflecting on the passage, I realized that "attending to His Word" and "keeping it in my heart" meant, in essence, to keep in focus what God says about a situation. Verse 22 tells us that "they" (God's words) are "life to those that find them, and health to all their flesh." I kept confessing, "Your Word within my heart is greater that any sickness." As I continued to confess this, my faith grew stronger.[71]

There came a point when I somehow knew in my heart that I was healed. There was no immediate physical evidence, but I felt a confident assurance. I can only describe it as a kind of inner knowing. I felt sure of God's Word and will and His provision for my healing. I got up, and before I reached the door, the migraine and all its symptoms were completely gone. Normally, I would have had to spend the rest of the day lying on a bed in a dark room, but this time, within ten minutes or so, it was gone. I left the room feeling empowered and confident in what is ours through putting our faith in Him.

Migraines did reoccur on two other occasions, but again I turned my focus on Jesus and His provision, and again the headaches lifted. That was over twenty years ago, and I have not had another migraine since then.

---

[71]   Proverbs 4:20–23.

When we experience or exercise this kind of faith, Paul calls it the "evidence" of things we desire but do not yet see.[72]

I began to realize that faith is much more than mental assent to truth. It's much more than holding to certain doctrinal creeds. It is also far superior to simply hoping and wishing for something. Faith is not merely a means to get something from God, and in this, we have sadly missed the point.

Faith is—or was intended to be—a way of life. It's a commitment to God and to His standards and perspective in light of Jesus's finished work.

We all have a portion of faith.[73] Paul called it the "measure of faith." No one has more faith or less faith than anyone else. We don't need more faith than we experienced at our initial salvation; it's the same faith. The truth is, a serious situation doesn't require more faith than a seemingly trivial issue.

When Jesus said to his disciples "oh you of little faith,"[74] He wasn't implying that they didn't have enough faith. The word *little* in the Greek is a word that means "puny," as in "weak" or "incredulous." Jesus assured us that all we need is a small amount of faith. Faith even as small as a mustard seed is capable of moving mountains.[75]

In this natural world, there are two ways that I know of to look at the things around us. The science of Newtonian physics studies the visible, tangible realm that consists of matter—animals, vegetation, and minerals and their interaction with such things as the law of gravity and aerodynamics—which we observe on a linear plain. And today, scientific studies have looked a little deeper and discovered that the physical world we can see and touch consists of a greater reality that we cannot see with our natural eyes.

The study of quantum physics tells us (among other things) that behind every cell and atom are energy and frequencies that, in a sense, hold them all together. In a study by Dr. James B. Richards, he talked about the fact that even our words generate frequencies, creating a harmonious or dissonant effect on our lives and even our health. It

---

72   Hebrews 11:1.

73   Romans 12:3.

74   Matthew 6:30.

75   Matthew 17:20.

amazes me to think that something invisible could have such a great effect on the visible world.

I'm not saying that this is the same thing, but as Christian believers, we must realize that there are two realms that we have access to. Sometimes we look at our circumstances and limit what God can do in our lives by our unbelief. Paul spoke of these two realities in his letter to the Corinthians. He said that there are two realms, or dimensions of reality, that we can know.[76]

There is what Paul calls the "seen" realm: the tangible, temporal, and changeable physical reality that we experience on this earth with our five senses. There is also an "unseen" realm of God's reality: His Word, principles, and character. According to scripture, the physical world is a reflection of God's character and His word made it and holds it together.[77]

Along the road of our lives, we often encounter various challenges. As believers, we stand, as it were, at a crossroads, a fork in the road. We are faced with the question of which reality will we trust in and identify with. Will we stand on what God's Word says or on what our experiences say?

On the one hand, there is the situation looming up before us. Sometimes the facts relentlessly and cruelly shout for our attention. We feel as though we have a right to be angry, a reason to worry, or a cause for fear. At times the situation can grab our attention, fill our thoughts, and drive our emotions until we are consumed by it. It's there when we wake up in the morning, and it's on our mind throughout the day—the symptoms and the doctor's report, the bills piling up, or the conflicts raging. It can all stand as a contradiction to God's Word and reality.

On the other hand, God's realm—His Word and His principles, promises, and provision—stand firm and immovable. This is God's reality, wherein all things are truly possible.[78] This is where the strength, the victory, the healing and health, and the solution we need are all readily available.

Faith is the essence of this new covenant; it is an integral part of our life in Christ. We see it in the gospel accounts, in Acts, and in the

---

[76]   Hebrews 11:3; 2 Corinthians 4:18.

[77]   Psalm 19:1; John 1:1–4; Hebrews 11:3; Romans 1:20.

[78]   Mark 10:27; 9:23.

epistles, where people experienced challenges such as sicknesses and disease, people in need, lack, a storm, and even prison. Through it all, they learned to choose to trust in another reality.

Jesus's earthly life was a demonstration of a man walking through this world—eating, drinking, laughing and crying, being hungry and tired—but with a focus on a greater reality and His needs supplied by a greater source.

Many times, people—even sometimes his disciples—misunderstood His words, for they were out of sync with His perspective.

Without faith it is impossible to please God, for when we continually consider the problems, we are removing God from the equation. It pleases Him when we dare to trust Him and take Him at His word.

When Peter stepped out of the boat,[79] the issue wasn't so much the miracle of walking on the water as it was his unwavering commitment in focusing on God's reality, regardless of the waves or the storm—or what his five senses were telling him. God's Word was his premise, and only when he considered his situation did he begin to sink.

You might say, "Margaret, you don't know the severity of my situation." That's true, I don't. If we live in this fallen world, we will encounter all kind of challenges, but the fact is that we are not victims if we are His.

Maybe you would say to me, "Are you implying that I can simply look at God and all my problems will go away—like Peter stepping out of the boat?"

Funny that you should say that, because in the historic account of Israel, we see thousands of people traveling through a desert and being bitten by poisonous snakes.[80] They fretted over their situation, and instead of trusting God, they complained and accused Him. Even though this problem was their own fault, God immediately took measures to provide a remedy. God instructed Moses to make a poisonous snake out of bronze and attach it to a pole. Anyone who had been bitten could just look—with expectation—at the pole and be healed.

We know in this new covenant time that Jesus's death on the cross destroyed the Devil and his right to operate in our lives. As we look to Jesus—that is, we turn our hearts to Him—we can expect to receive

---

[79]   Matthew 14:28–30.

[80]   Numbers 21:4–9.

our healing and take hold of His provision. As blood-bought believers, we now have a legal right to live in peace, prosperity, and victory in our lives and to take hold of the healing, health, and wholeness that we have need of.

Like Peter, our commitment, regardless of our present experience, has to be to trust in Him. The waves may be swelling and the wind raging, and the situation might seem impossible or hopeless, with no solution in sight. But if we dare to believe and take Him at His word, He will never fail us.

Timothy described it well when he said that we must "fight the good fight of faith and lay hold on eternal life."[81]

In the Greek, the word translated as "good" is actually the word *beautiful*. From God's perspective, it is a beautiful thing when we choose, regardless of circumstances, to trust His Word.

---

[81]   1 Timothy 6:12.

CHAPTER 19

Core Stability

The Lord said to Samuel, "Look not on the countenance or on the
height of his stature … for the Lord sees not as man sees, for man
looks on the outward appearance,
but the Lord looks on the heart."
—1 Samuel 16:7

Have you ever had lower back pain? I have. Working in the garden
and doing a lot of bending always aggravates the problem. I've often
reached a point where I can barely straighten up again. Consequently,
I have spent many a day on the couch with a hot-water bottle on my
back and a bottle of Ibuprofen beside me. Lower back pain can be
debilitating.

A few years ago, a began a series of visits to a physiotherapist.
There I discovered the root of the problem: I had weak core muscles.
The combination of not-so-good posture and weak core muscles was an
accident waiting to happen, and it did.

There are muscle groups that run down and across the back that act
as a support for the spine and pelvis. Instability in these core muscles
will result in weakness in the mobilizing muscles of the arms and legs.
Similarly, the apostle Paul admonished us to "gird up the loins with
truth.".[82] (The "loins" could also refer to the core muscles of the pelvis.
Of course, we understand that he was using this illustration in speaking
of the mind.

---

[82]   Ephesians 6:10.

In Paul's time, going into battle meant that each soldier had to be strong and capable of running and wielding a spear. A girdle made of firmly woven materials and wrapped around the pelvis would have supported the core muscles. As well, the breastplate, though worn for protection, may also have produced a stabilizing effect, thus facilitating strength of movement to the arms and legs.

So, what does all this have to do with our walk with the Lord? It has everything to do with it. Core stability is an amazing picture of the most important part of the Christian life. It's an area we often tend to minimize, overlooking its significance.

How is your core? You may have extensive knowledge of scripture, or maybe you have exercised great faith at times, but when you are faced with troubling circumstances, do you waver and wonder? You might live a good Christian life and try hard to do the right thing, but when you fail, are you beaten down with condemnation? Maybe you have a core issue.

I'm not talking about doctrinal foundations or even great faith. I'm referring to the very root of our lives, which is the heart. If this core is not stable, healthy, and strong, we will spend our lives on a roller coaster of spiritual highs and lows, never coming to a stable, productive Christian life.

The Greek word *kar-dee-a*, taken from a root meaning "core, center, or middle," is the English word *heart*. This word in the Greek represents the innermost part, the very core of our being. This is who I am, the real me. Paul called it "the inner man of the heart."

This may not necessarily match the image you present to the world. A least, there is more to you than what people see externally. We may act a certain way, but often our motives, inner thoughts, and feelings are not reflected externally. The heart is the deep, inner, secret, honest, naked, unpretentious you. This is who God sees and relates to.

God doesn't have to shout down out of heaven to us. Rarely does He speak to us in an audible voice in this new covenant. He speaks in the "secret place" of our individual hearts.[83] Jesus, speaking against the Pharisees' long, showy public prayers, told his disciples, "When you pray, enter into your closet, and when you have shut the door, pray to your Father which is in secret." The Greek meaning of the phrase *in secret* speaks of words such as *concealed*, *private*, *hidden*, and *inward*. If

---

[83] Psalm 91:1; Matthew 6:6.

we're not settled in the new covenant, we'll continue trying to pray to God as if He were far away in heaven. Though He resides far above and superior to the limited realm of earth, His Spirit now lives within us.

In 1 Kings 19:11–12, we see the prophet Elijah in a dire situation, seeking God. In this account, Elijah went up onto a mountain. There, a great wind arose, so forceful that it broke away some of the rock on the side of the mountain. Then we read that "God was not in the wind." After that, there occurred an earthquake, but the passage tells us that God wasn't in the earthquake. After the earthquake, there was a fire, and again scripture tells us that God wasn't in the fire. Even at a time before the Holy Spirit was given, when God spoke to mankind only through specially anointed prophets and signs, God demonstrated, through Elijah's experience on the mountain, His ultimate intention for His relationship with mankind.

Many Christians seek after great manifestations of the Spirit or crave miracles, signs, and wonders, but less often do we set aside time to commune with God in the secret place of our hearts.

If you don't often hear Him in this way, it could be that you are not accustomed to listening with your heart, or maybe you are unaware that this is possible. He is always speaking if we are willing to hear.

When I was a young Christian, there were times when I sought God for various needs. Sometimes my prayers were somewhat shallow; I'd go through the motions of laying out my requests as I had observed others doing. Then I'd get up and go my way, hoping that He would answer in some way.

As time went on, I began to realize that prayer had to be much more than that. In fact, there was a growing desire in my heart for a greater reality in prayer. It wasn't so much my own desire to pray, but the Holy Spirit was drawing me to fellowship with the Father, just as Jesus taught that He would.[84]

We don't have to shout or even speak audibly for Him to hear us. We don't have to perform to impress Him or get His attention. When we pray publicly, there is a tendency to guard and orchestrate our words. We don't have to be "Toastmasters" or poets, and we don't need to measure our words or speak in King James's English when we talk with our Father. There is nothing to compare with "closet prayer"—that is, fellowship with God in the secret place of our hearts.

---

[84] Matthew 6:6.

In Psalm 27:14, David said, "Wait on the Lord, be of good courage, and He shall strengthen your heart." The word translated here as "wait" is a Hebrew word that means "to bind together, to expect," which denotes the idea of clinging to something with expectation, rather than just hanging around passively. For the believer, prayer is more than sending out requests; it must be a connection with God in our hearts. Only this kind of prayer can produce change in a heart.

The truth is, God is concerned about the state of our hearts. The heart is the center of a Christian's life. It's God's "meeting place" with each of us. It's the focal point of His working in our lives.

When we talk about the "state of the heart," our religious thinking brings to mind terms such as *evil, deceitful, wicked,* and *in need of contrition and repentance.* This is old covenant thinking with religious concepts that are not in line with what Jesus has done for us. In this new covenant time, God's focus is not, as we sometimes assume, on making us "right" with Him, for Jesus has, through His death, burial, and resurrection, already dealt with the sin issue. We must believe this and accept it. This new covenant is not about making us "right," but it is, first and foremost, focused on making us *whole* so that we can live this righteous new life.

After Jesus called Matthew to follow Him,[85] He sat at the table in Matthew's house, and many other tax collectors and sinners joined them. When the Pharisees saw this, they indignantly said to the disciples, "Why does your teacher eat with tax collectors and sinners?" Jesus, hearing this, said to them, "Those who are well have no need of a physician, but those that are sick." He continued and added, "Go and learn what this means: 'I desire mercy and not sacrifice'[86] … for I did not come to call the righteous, but sinners, to repentance." Apparently Jesus recognized that the sinners' deeds were not necessarily the issue, but sickness of the heart was.

Isaiah spoke on this very subject in His prophecy,[87] and we know that Jesus, when He began His ministry, read from this very passage.[88]

---

85   Matthew 9:8–13.

86   Hosea 6:6.

87   Isaiah 61:1.

88   Luke 6:18.

He chose this particular passage for a specific reason. It was truly a fitting introduction to the start of His earthly ministry.

Isaiah's prophecy is as follows: "The spirit of the Lord God is upon me; because He has anointed me to proclaim the good news onto the meek. He has sent me to bind up the brokenhearted, to proclaim liberty to the captives and the opening of the prison to them that are bound, and to proclaim the acceptable year of the Lord."[89]

Jesus read it this way: "The spirit of the Lord is upon me, because He has anointed me to preach the gospel to the poor; He has sent me to heal the brokenhearted, to preach deliverance to the captives and recovering of sight to the blind, to set at liberty them that are bruised. To preach the acceptable year of the Lord."[90]

At this point, Jesus rolled up the scroll and sat down. All eyes were upon him, and He said to them, "This day is this scripture fulfilled in your ears."[91]

Jesus was the one who would deal with the core issue and reach down, as it were, to the very root of our problem: our hearts.

In the Greek, the word *poor* (or in Hebrew, the word *meek*) speaks of "depressed, humble, and needy." In this case, the reference was toward an internal state—the condition of our hearts—rather than an external state—the financially poor.

From the beginning of creation and throughout history, God has looked upon mankind and has seen beyond the outward manifestations of sin and its workings. He has seen the heart of man and his fallen state. Those whom He intended to be royalty, kings and priests clothed in dignity and honor, were now crouching and cringing in fear, bowed down as beggars under oppression, distress, and calamity.[92] Yes, man was in sin and separated from God, thus living in poverty and lack and under the oppression of sickness of the soul and body.

When we realize that the heart is the very root of the problem of sin and all its effects, we can say more accurately that sin is only a symptom of a deeper problem. It wouldn't be presumptuous to say that God is concerned about restoring wholeness and stability to our hearts.

---

[89]   Isaiah 61:1.

[90]   Luke 4:18.

[91]   Luke 4:21.

[92]   As indicated by both the Hebrew and Greek, *Strong's Exhaustive Concordance.*

Wouldn't you agree that the whole world is broken from the inside out? People—both believers and unbelievers—drift through life carrying their heartaches, sorrows, and generations of dysfunction. It's no wonder that wars, crime, poverty, and destruction are all around us.

Genesis says that after the fall of man "God saw that the wickedness of man was great in the earth, and every imagination of the thoughts was only evil continually."[93]

The word translated as "wickedness" is a Hebrew word that means "adversity, affliction, calamity, distress, evil (favored), misery, sadness, trouble, and wretchedness." This creates an image very different from our religious perspective. Not only did sin and evil abound, but God, who sees and searches the heart, saw the miserable, troubled state of men's hearts, thoughts, and perceptions, which produced their sinful actions.

Ezekiel told us that "the heart is deceitful and desperately wicked."[94] Here we see that the word translated into English as "wicked" is the Hebrew word for *melancholy*, and the word translated as "deceitful" is a Hebrew word meaning "troubled."

We try to make ourselves "right" with God from the outside first by concentrating on reforming our deeds. God's method is to make us "whole"—from the inside first. Whole people can make right decisions; they can live as God intended, because they can accept God's love and recognize their new identity in Him. Broken people cannot choose the good; their perspective of God, themselves, and life is distorted. They cannot grasp what Jesus has done for them, for all they can see is their own weaknesses, failure, and unworthiness.

It's true that our problem is internal, in our hearts, but God, who searches the heart and knows our needs before we even ask, freely offers us the solution.

---

[93]   Genesis 6:5–6.

[94]   The King James Version.

CHAPTER 20

A Trusting Relationship

"This is eternal life, that they might know You,
the only true God and Jesus Christ whom You have sent."
—John 17:3

We all know many things about God. There are, I would guess, thousands of books, Bible studies, and messages from the pulpit based on the subject.

The real question, though, is: do we really know Him? Knowing *about* someone is quite different from actually being well acquainted personally.

Intellectual knowledge is good and can be useful in factual research, but in the challenges of daily life, having information about God is not enough. Our faith is encouraged when we read accounts of those who have experienced God's love, comfort, guidance, and help, but it's far more challenging to trust Him when it comes down to our own circumstances and needs. How can we trust Him if we don't know Him?

Religious thinking has caused us to believe that intimacy with God is something reserved for the mystics, ascetics, or a special, anointed few. But for the believer, knowing God in a personal way should be the norm.

Ultimately, the whole point of the Christian life is a personal and trusting relationship. When we don't recognize this fact, we are easily distracted and preoccupied with many (even good) things, and we neglect the most important thing.

Jesus said, "Except you abide in Me, you cannot bear fruit."[95] The Amplified Bible says it this way: "Unless you remain intimately and vitally united with Me" and live your life out of this reality, all your efforts will not produce what you desire.

One day Jesus went up onto a mountain with His disciples, apart from the multitudes, and taught them many things. At one point he said, "Not everyone who calls me Lord, shall enter the kingdom of heaven, but he that does the will of the Father."[96] As I mentioned earlier in this book, I believe that he was not just referring to entering heaven when we die. I believe he was saying that entering the kingdom is about experiencing the realities of God's provision in our personal experience here on earth.

Jesus talked with his disciples about many people who would do great things in His name, but then He added, "I will declare to them, 'I never knew you; depart from me.'"

The disciples must have thought, *What? What does He mean?* Surely all the good things they were doing were what Jesus called "doing the will of the Father." But apparently that was not the case, because according to this passage, the Father's will was for them to know Him. The truth is, it's only through an ongoing, vital relationship with God that we can consistently bear good fruit in our lives.

I remember the first few months after I had come to the Lord. I'd wake up in the morning excited about life. I'd be looking for opportunities to serve Him. I was motivated and filled with joy, confident that He was always there with me. That was the thing that inspired me.

Instead of striving to do good works while remaining uncertain about His will, our lives can be an expression of a hearing relationship. He wants to guide and direct our lives and decisions by His Spirit within us, speaking to our hearts. This is what relationship with God is about.

Jesus Himself taught and demonstrated a relationship with God throughout His earthly life. He deliberately took time alone daily to commune with the Father. Mark mentioned this in his account when he said, "In the morning, rising up a great while before day, he [Jesus] went out, and departed into a solitary place, and there prayed."[97]

---

[95] John 15:4.

[96] Matthew 7:21–23.

[97] Mark 1:35.

One day, in a prayer to His Father, Jesus said, "This is eternal life, that they might know You, the only true God, and Jesus Christ whom You have sent." It's clear that this quality of life given to believers involves knowing Him in personal experience. Wouldn't you like to experience this eternal, abundant life[98] that Jesus came to give us? We do, in fact, have access to this kind of life through this unique relationship.

When Jesus returned to the Father, He left us the Holy Spirit, just as He had promised. The Spirit was the one who was to be "with us" and "in us."[99] Jesus said of Himself, "I will not leave you comfortless; I will come to you." Some believe that this is only in reference to "initial salvation when we first come to Christ, but I believe that this was meant to be an ongoing and necessary part of our lives here on earth.

Jesus spoke at great length on this subject. He said, "I am in the Father and the Father is in me," and He went on to explain that the words He spoke and the works He did were not by His own efforts or abilities but by the direction, inspiration, and empowerment that was His through His connection with the Father.[100]

In another place, Jesus explained, "He that believes on me, the works that I do shall he do also and greater,"[101] and this through our relationship with Him.

Jesus told His disciples that when the Holy Spirit came to dwell in them, they would know and understand this unique relationship that He had with the Father.

Even Paul made reference to this when he spoke of our having received the "spirit of adoption," whereby we can sense a witness in our hearts, recognizing God as our Father.[102]

In another place, Paul gave expression to the yearnings of his own heart when he said, "That I might know Him."[103]

The very heart of the Christian life is a personal, intimate, and ongoing relationship with God.

---

[98]   John 10:10.

[99]   John 17:3, 20–22.

[100]   John 14:10.

[101]   John 14:12–13.

[102]   Romans 8:15.

[103]   Philippians 3:10.

In the beginning, we see Adam and Eve walking in the garden with God. Their whole life revolved around their relationship with God. Adam's abilities, his wisdom in naming the animals and managing the earth and the environment, and even the name *Eden* (which means "delight") help us to grasp the sheer pleasure and joy that encompassed their lives. Certainly, every part of their experience was a reflection of this wonderful relationship they had with God.

Every Christian is familiar with the phrase *relationship with God*, but many are uncertain and vague as to what it really means in personal experience.

To begin, we have to rid ourselves of our religious, old covenant concepts about relating to God. They bind us to the idea that God is mysterious or aloof, and then we never know what He might do or how He might respond. If, even after the new birth, we perceive God in view of our sinful, fallen state, then a relationship with Him as our Father eludes us. We must first be grounded in the gospels, established in the reality of God's love and integrity, and settled on Jesus's teachings and life example. Before we can grasp the reality of this relationship with God, we must put down our roots and understand what His provision— His death, burial, and resurrection—really means for us.

The English word *relationship* doesn't adequately define what this connection with God really means. It's much more than intellectual knowledge about Him. It's far greater than a casual acquaintance or occasional interaction. For the new covenant believer, this vital connection with God through His Spirit within our hearts is far superior to any relationship. It can have a positive effect on every area of our lives. We were designed to live in constant communion with the eternal one, like a branch to a vine. He is "nearer than breathing," someone once said.

Fellowship with God wasn't meant to be a complicated, arduous task requiring great amounts of dedicated time, fasting, and self-denial. There is nothing wrong with spending much time (if you can) or putting aside distractions (as with fasting), but it's not about earning points with God or putting in time. There are no set rules to follow. Simply said, if you want to get to know someone, you must spend time together.

Relationship with God is more than prayer—in the traditional sense of kneeling by your bed—but as believers we must recognize that we always have access to Him. We can expect Him to be there every time we turn our focus to Him in faith. John tells us that we can know by faith that He hears us when we pray. We have this confidence because of Jesus.

On a natural level, studies have shown that children who grow up in a loving, accepting, nurturing environment possess an inner sense of personal validity, confidence, and value. While going through the teen years, they may experience their share of self-doubt, but regardless of the challenges and wrong decisions along the way, they will generally go through life with a stabilizing sense of dignity.

On the other hand, those who grow up without experiencing a supportive and loving environment tend to be more prone to personal doubt, intimidation, and caving in to peer pressure as youths. Even as adults they carry with them this sense of lack. I'm sure there are exceptions, some who have overcome these things, but the fact remains that we were designed to be loved.

How much more, then, would a personal realization of God's love for us and valuing of us bring greater stability and a healthy sense of self to our lives, regardless of the childhood environment?

I grew up in a troubled and unsettled environment that was not entirely secure or nurturing, and I took on beliefs about myself that were not true. I know that Mum loved me, as did my dad, but their love was not easily expressed in such a difficult situation, and in my limited understanding as a child, I assumed that I was unlovable or unworthy.

I carried these feelings with me into adult life, and they had a negative effect on my life, my friends, and all my endeavors. I had few close friends, and many times I forfeited career opportunities. In spite of my abilities and qualifications, self-doubt held me back. It wasn't until I came to finally realize God's love for me that I was able to shed the shackles of my faulty beliefs.

As a young believer—and over the years that followed—I often found comfort and encouragement in reading the Psalms. In many ways, I could identify with David. Of course, I never had a javelin thrown at me, and I never had to flee for my life, but through this life I have encountered troubling circumstances, as we all do. I have wrestled with fears and worries, and I have even felt far away from God at times.

In reading the Psalms, we sometimes find David discouraged or overwhelmed by his situation. In the early part of Psalm 77, David went into great detail about the severity of his problem. In verse 2, he said, "I complained and my heart was overwhelmed." How true this is! When we focus on the problem, it becomes magnified in our thinking, and our faith goes out the window.

At one point, David asked, "Will the Lord cast off forever? and will He be favorable no more? Is His mercy gone forever? Do His promises fail? Has God forgotten to be gracious? or has He in anger shut up His mercies?"[104] How many times have you asked similar questions in a difficult time?

There was a time in my own life when I struggled with fear and anxiety. I'd wake up during the night with my heart pounding, gripped with fear. It was horrible. In the course of time, I discovered that it had stemmed from a particular incident I had experienced as a child. It had lodged in my heart. I found that certain situations—unrelated but similar to the original incident—would bring on the same feeling with the same intensity. The Lord began to show me the power of His Word. I began to meditate on (think about) and confess (talk about) God's love for me, His desire for my health and stability, and Jesus's provision toward that end. In each situation, I learnt to turn my heart and the focus my attention on His love. Soon I began to recognize His presence with me and to believe the value that He has for me. After some time of doing this I was completely free.

You can't hear His words of comfort and guidance in your heart if your heart is already full of worry, fear, and doubt. We can't take hold of the help He longs to give us if we're distracted with the problem.

Now that we know that God never sends trouble to test, purify, or teach us, we can trust Him in the face of difficulties. We can know that His will always leads us out of trouble and into victory, which He has already wrought for us through Jesus. Praise God! When we think of Jesus, we can understand God's will for us.

In difficult times, we must hold on to His Word and all the more put our trust in Him. Troubles come to steal the Word from our hearts and undermine our trust in God. When we stand on His Word, we become established and strong. This is a vital component of a relationship with God.

But finally, like the Prodigal Son, David came to himself and said in verse 6, "I call to remembrance my song in the night. I commune with my own heart: and my spirit made diligent search. I will remember

---

[104] Psalm 77:1–20.

the works of the Lord." In verse 12, David said, "I will meditate also on all Thy works and talk of all Your doings." Suddenly David's whole perspective changed, and he was no longer just talking about the Lord but was communing with Him. At first he was just remembering the works of the Lord, but in the end he said, "I will meditating on and talk about Your works."

In another Psalm, we see David worshipping God in trusting abandon.[105] This can be the prevailing attitude of any child of God. Regardless of our situation or the problem we are facing, we can know that He is trustworthy and always near to help.[106]

After all, it's really all about trust. Trust is the foundation of a lasting, quality relationship.

I believe that trust was the thing that was lost at the fall. Sure, Adam and Eve disobeyed God's instruction, but something deeper and more insidious took place there. A man and a woman were tempted to compromise their trust in God and His Word. The Devil sowed a seed of doubt with a few simple questions: "Did He really mean that you would actually die? Perhaps He's withholding some good and beneficial thing from you."[107] These were the essence of the lie that that tore mankind out of the place where all his needs were met and his deepest desires were fulfilled, the place of relationship with almighty God. In their hearts, God's integrity was in question, and trust was broken.

Whether we're going through hard times or living everyday life, we can keep our hearts in tune with Him. Just as a deer is alert to the slightest sound and pricks up its ears at a moment's notice, so we can cultivate such a hearing relationship.

If you're witnessing to someone, you can silently pray, "Lord, give me wisdom. Guide my words." And He will.

One day I was driving to work and was ready to pull out onto a busy highway. I automatically looked to the left and then to the right. I was about to pull out, when the thought came within me to look again. I did, and seemingly out of nowhere, a semitruck came barreling down the highway.

---

[105] Psalm 150.

[106] Hebrews 4:16.

[107] Genesis 3:4–5.

Another time I was on my way to a friend's house. I had promised to water her plants while she was away. I was just about go out the door, when I had a feeling that I was forgetting something. I was in a hurry, though, because my friend lived a distance away, and I had several other things I had to do around town, so I put aside the feeling and continued on my way.

When I got to the door of my friend's house, I realized what it was that I had forgotten. I had taken a different purse and had not checked to make sure the keys were in it. Consequently, I had to drive all the way back home to get the keys and then return. Walking with God is about learning to recognize the still, small voice of the Holy Spirit in our hearts within the practical experiences of our daily lives.

The point is that we're not down here slugging it out on our own. We don't have to carry our burdens alone or trudge through life's difficulties as best we can. There's no performing, no striving, and no irksome obligation; there's just the opportunity for an intimate, personal, life-changing relationship with God, our Father, who knows us infinitely and loves us more than we can fathom. We can trust Him because He is trustworthy.

How wonderful it is to know that this kind of relationship is available to us day by day! Walking in this way can fill us with peace and confidence through all of life's challenges. Learning to hear His voice and follow His direction fills our lives with great purpose and satisfaction. Then we find that our lives take on greater significance as we realize our new identity in Him.

CHAPTER 21

Identity: A New Creation

"You're not who you think you are, you're not who others think
you are, and you're not who you think others think you are."
—James B. Richards,

We have to know who we are in order to have a healthy sense of self.
We must have a realistic and accurate evaluation of ourselves, especially
as believers, if we want to succeed in life and connect with people and
make a difference.

Some of us have an image we try to portray, but it may not reflect
our real self. It's a rare individual who is who he seems to be, regardless
of where he is or with whom. My husband is one of these people. John
is himself, regardless of the situation. He is secure in who he is, and
rarely is he intimidated by other people.

A pastor of a church we once attended used to say, "I have nothing to
hide, nothing to prove, and nothing to lose."[108] What a truly liberating
statement!

Some people change with every encounter. Insecure in themselves,
they are always performing or conforming for acceptance, sometimes
even to the extent that they drive people away because no one really
knows who they are. We must be true to ourselves!

There are some people whose philosophy is: "I am who I am, and if
you don't like it, that's your problem." They exude a degree of confidence,
but their input is of little value to anyone because they just don't care.

---

[108]   Pastor Don Richmond, Hockey Ministry, Evangel Church, Kelowna, B.C.

The way you see yourself is a crucial issue. It affects every part of your life. Even as babies in the womb, our sense of self was being formed and affected by the thoughts and feelings of our mother. Even before we could understand spoken words, we perceived in our environment the feelings and attitudes around us. Our beliefs about ourselves—whether or not we are lovable, unlovable, valued and significant, or worthless and of little consequence—become an unspoken question that we carry with us throughout our lives until we settle the matter within ourselves.

This matter of self-worth can have an influence on every area of our lives: our success or failure in relationships, the things we pursue, our happiness, and even our health.

Individuals may have earned several diplomas and certificates and may possess all the skills needed to qualify for a particular position, but if they don't feel good about themselves or are insecure regarding their abilities, chances are that they won't get the job they are applying for. How we see ourselves communicates more than our education or training. If you are not confident, how can a potential employer put his confidence in you?

Our sense of self has so much to do with our perception of how God sees us. We accumulate all kinds of concepts of God's estimation of us, and these may or may not be accurate or scripturally based. Regardless, we tend to hold on to them.

Years ago, my husband attended a Jehovah's Witnesses church with a friend he was hoping to enlighten. They had a communion service, which was their regular practice. They passed around the bread and a cup of wine, and each person in turn declined to partake, confessing his unworthiness. This is a sad picture in view of what Jesus has done for us. Yet we too, though we express it differently, sometimes relate to God in a similar way.

One would expect that the average Christian would be stable in the matter of self-worth, but unfortunately, this is not always the case.

Dr. Richards addresses this issue well when he says, "Sadly, there are actually churches that nurture low self-worth as if it had some spiritual value." I know this to be a fact, because I was once part of such a church. I had serious self-worth issues even before I joined this church.

As I mentioned earlier, my dad was unable to connect with my brother and me on any emotional level because of his illness. I tried to perform or comply in order to gain acceptance with him. I even learned to like buttermilk just to gain his approval. This attitude carried over into my young adult life to some degree.

Someone at the fellowship church once commended me as an example of spirituality because of my quiet and withdrawn demeanor at the time. Whether I was spiritual or not, this person's method of measurement wasn't based on New Testament standards.

We tend to judge on the surface, and we assume that God does too. We see people in terms of their actions, good works, or sinful deeds, and we expect God to judge in reaction to this as well. God's focus is the heart, and He understands our inner thoughts and needs.

Many Christians get nervous and twitchy when they hear the term *self-worth*. They associate this term with psychology, humanism, or maybe just the thinking of "the world." Sometimes the world stands head and shoulders above us in recognizing our internal needs. Yet ironically, we actually hold the solution to those very needs through our identity in Christ.

We've been taught that God sees us as fallen, sinful, and unworthy, so we conclude that He expects us to live in a humble, lowly, unassuming way and to remain weak and powerless, not realizing our value before God and the abundant provision that is ours in Christ. We are all very much aware of our old tendencies, shortcomings, and weaknesses, and we identify with this lie to the point that its limiting effects overflow into our lives.

At the fellowship church, I came to believe that it was pleasing to God when I beat myself up by condemning myself for my shortcomings. Maybe I assumed it showed Him how humble I was. I continued in this misconception until someone introduced me to the "good news" of God's love and the value He places on us. I had already come to know the Lord a few years prior to this, and I had known and trusted His love for me. Contrary teaching within the context of the fellowship had caused me to forget this important truth. It was through the taped messages of James B. Richards that I began to realize the value God placed on me, and I had no right to see myself any other way.

We know that God doesn't want us to be inflated with conceit or to try to appear superior to others or arrogant, which the Greek indicates is the word *pride*. The truth is, He want us to know with confidence who we are in Him.

True humility accepts God's love and approval apart from our own efforts and merit.[109] True meekness is not weakness but controlled strength. Paul told us that God's love constrains us; that is, according to the Greek, it holds us, keeps us in, and compels us to live a righteous life.[110]

We have learned to look into the scriptures to find out what is wrong with us, and we look to the law to evaluate what we are doing wrong and where we fall short. This old covenant mentality keeps us striving to please God and laboring to make or keep ourselves right with God by our works. Thus we are never being sure where we stand or if we are good enough.

Even after Christ has come into our lives, we still assume that we are the same old person—except that we are forgiven. I used to think this way, assuming I was merely a "saved sinner" who was doing the best I could and waiting for my change in heaven.

No! The truth is that if I am in Christ, I am a new creation *now*. Nowhere in scripture does it say that I am part old creation and part new.

Contrary to popular religious belief, we are not living with a dual nature. According to Paul's writings, our old man, or person, is in fact dead. He made the issue very clear when he said, regarding the representation of water baptism, "Do you not know that as many of us as were baptized into Christ Jesus were baptized into his death? Therefore we were buried with him through baptism into death, that just as Christ was raised from the dead by the glory of the Father, even so we also should walk in newness of life."[111]

Everything in the new covenant involves a walk of faith. If God says something, it's not our prerogative to try to second-guess Him about what He really means or to construct some man-made theory to prop up our unbelief. Some people purport that we are a "new creation" only in a "positional" or perhaps "spiritual" way. If God says it, it's so. If Jesus did it, it's done.

At the time of our initial salvation, we don't throw it back at God and say, "I don't feel saved," or "I'm still tempted to sin, so this 'new

---

[109]   Ephesians 1:6; 3:12; 1:4

[110]   2 Corinthians 5:14.

[111]   Romans 6:4 NKJV.

birth' can't really be true," or "perhaps I'll be saved and my sins forgiven when I get to heaven." No! We walk by faith.

If you have believed and accepted this reality, you are now a new creation, and you have a new identity. God is not trying to ignore your old nature. He considers it to be dead and you to be alive in Christ. That's how God sees it.

God is not interested in patching up, growing up, or improving the old person. There is no need to ask Him to give you more patience, or to make you more loving, or even to take away or deal with your pride or anger problem. All that I am and all that I need is in Him.

Paul told us, "Set your mind on things above, and not on things on the earth. For you died, and your life is hidden with Christ, in God."[112] He also said, "I have been crucified with Christ; it is no longer I that live, but Christ lives in me; and the life which I now live in the flesh I live by the faith of the Son of God, who loved me and gave himself for me."[113] So now we can say without contradiction, "I am a new person in Christ. I have a new nature, a regenerated heart, and an awakened conscience within me."

If we have accepted Jesus into our lives, then we must see ourselves as He sees us. We must understand that water baptism is an illustration of what actually happened at the new birth. Not only were our sins forgiven, but they were taken away. Jesus became both Savior and Lord, and He gave us a new identity. Water baptism is also a declaration before man and God of one's intent to live this new life in relationship with Christ.

It's all about being "in Christ." This is not just in a legal or theological standing; it is an actual, present reality. We have to acknowledge God's point of view based on what Jesus has accomplished for us.

I know; we don't always act like new creations, do we? But this is who God says we are. Before Christ came to the earth, we were bound by the nature we inherited from Adam—a fallen, carnal, limited, faithless, sinful nature. Paul told us that when Christ rose from the dead, we were in Him. Now we are no longer bound by the limitations of Adam, but we are risen into newness of life to walk on this earth and bear witness of His provision.

---

[112] Colossians 3:3.

[113] Galatians 2:20.

It's a walk of faith, after all, and day by day we must learn to say no to the old tendencies toward anger, fear, depression, doubt, and so on. We must cultivate the habit of turning our hearts and thoughts to the reality of who we are in Him because of Jesus.

One important aspect of dying to self is the "putting off" (letting go of, disassociating with) the old nature[114] and "putting on" the new. When I identify with the new person, it's not a case of behavior modification by my efforts. I find that as I yield to Christ in me, it just flows out of my heart, and I naturally want to do the right thing.

Until we realize how He sees us and our intrinsic worth to Him, personally and individually, we cannot deny ourselves. We can only drawback in fear, self-protection, and self-justification as Job did, always trying to justify ourselves.

When I identify with the old person, I can only relate to God through my own efforts, because from this perspective, I can only see myself as sinful and separated from God. Dying to self is, in my own strength, an arduous and impossible task.

Don't waste your time trying to be a better person; simply yield to the new nature. Certainly, if you have a problem with some sin—such as stealing, lusting, gossiping, or any other sin—you should put yourself under the law or make the effort not to do those things. That's better than wrecking your life or someone else's, or hardening your heart against God. But learning to yield to the new nature within you is a far better way.

The word *yield* means "to give way, to submit or surrender to, or to cede"—that is, to give up or hand over rule to another. Yielding to the new nature is not about striving to perform like a good Christian should; it is about surrendering to the new nature within. When you're driving down a road and you see a triangular sign marked "Yield," it means that you must give up the right of way to a certain lane of traffic or to pedestrians. We give them priority and let them go first.

Several years ago, I was working part time as a cook in a restaurant. One particular coworker and myself just could not seem to get along, and we were often running into conflict. One day it came to a head, and we raised our voices and exchanged angry words. I can't even remember exactly what we were arguing about, but her attitude smacked of arrogance, and before I could even think it through, I had slapped her

---

114   Ephesians 4:22; Colossians 3:8–9; Galatians 3:27; Ephesians 4:24.

across the face. We stood there, silent and wide-eyed, like deer caught in the headlights, staring at each other. I think I was as shocked as she was. The problem wasn't resolved there, but we both left, troubled.

That evening, I prayed for myself and also for my coworker Jane. Before that, the thought had never even crossed my mind to pray for her, but as I did so, I became aware of a different feeling in my heart toward her. Later, we talked over coffee. I apologized, and she did too. The animosity was gone, and in its place was a love beyond my natural tendencies. The moment I chose to pray for her was a step in the process of yielding to the new righteous nature.

When we choose to identify ourselves with the old nature and just go with the old way of thinking and reacting, we are resisting the new life within us, and in our unbelief, we are hindering what God would do in our lives.

When I lose sight of the reality of my new identity and seem to fall short, there is no condemnation. Though we would condemn ourselves, the Holy Spirit convicts us of righteousness and reminds us of who we are: righteous and beloved sons and daughters of God in Christ.

Joseph Prince[115] explains to us that the Holy Spirit, who now indwells us, was sent to convict us of righteousness.[116] This is not to rebuke or condemn us for our unrighteousness but to convict and convince us of the righteousness that is now in us through Christ.[117]

As in James's illustrations,[118] I'm like a person looking in a mirror. When I spend time in God's presence and read and ponder the scriptures, I'm encouraged and find a witness in my heart that affirms the reality that I am a new person with a new identity in Christ. Then I go my way and get distracted by the challenges of life, and I begin to see myself as I was before Christ. I do not apply His Word in my experience or put it into practice in my life, and as a consequence, I forget who I really am in Christ.

The identity crisis is over! No more false humility or self-destructive, Christ-denying views of ourselves. We are righteous and beloved sons and daughters of the Most High God. I now have a new sense of self,

---

[115] Joseph Prince, *Destined to Reign*, Harrison House Publishers, 86.

[116] John 16:7–10.

[117] Romans 5:17; Ephesians 4:24.

[118] James 1:22–25.

a sense of honor and dignity. You and I are new creations that never existed before. We live on this earth with eternity dwelling in our hearts, and we possess a new capacity to live in fellowship with God as we walk on this earth.

CHAPTER 22

Well Equipped: A True Perspective

"We all have *extraordinary* encoded within us, waiting to be released."
—Jean Houston

I have to admit that it troubles and perplexes me to hear of Christians—those for whom Christ died and then wrought so great a victory—living in fear and uncertainty, powerless and often defeated, just putting up with whatever life brings their way as though they were victims.

Ted had worked as a roofer for many years, and one day he lost his footing and fell. He was a strong Christian and an active member of a church, but his first reaction to the accident was, "My back is shot, and I don't know what we're going to do. I guess I'll have to go on compensation." The church prayed for him, his wife, and his three small children, asking God to be near to them during this trial." Some kind woman offered to babysit so that the wife could work part time. People were kind and caring, but no one ever alluded to Jesus's provision for healing and restoration.

One morning, Janice asked for prayer at a ladies' Bible study. Her husband, though a good father and loving husband, was an alcoholic. He had a hard time keeping a job, and they were deep in debt. Their fifteen-year-old son was in trouble with the law. He and three friends had robbed and vandalized a store. On top of that, her daughter had just been diagnosed with a serious food allergy. One woman advised Janice to accept these thing from God's hand as a vehicle for building

Christian character. In spite of the fact that she was a believer and living under the new covenant, no one told her that God was willing to meet all her needs.[119]

Years ago, I knew a young man who, though highly intelligent and a serious Christian, lived in fear. He watched the news religiously every evening, taking note of what was going on. He talked often about natural disasters and falling meteorites. He was well informed about the many wars going on around the world and about terrorist groups. He studied various epidemics and viruses. He had a collection of books on what to do in case of a nuclear attack and how to build a fallout shelter. He had surrounded himself with proactive resources, but he was living in fear and uncertainty. He had overlooked the fact that now, in Christ, he could say like David, "Though a host should encamp against me, my heart shall not fear. Though war should rise against me, in this will I be confident."[120] He could have realized, as the apostle Paul did, that God has given us supernatural[121] power rather than a spirit of fear.

Why do we settle for so much less than what God has given us? I do it, and so do you. Every time we look at the problem and forget who we are, we forfeit what He has given us.

Andrew Wommack asked, "Did you know that a Christian can actually die from sickness or disease while the same power that raised Jesus from the dead lies dormant within him? Or did you know that believers can be overcome with depression, anger, and bitterness, all the while possessing God's love, joy, and peace in their spirit?"[122]

I'm convinced that many Christians still believe that God wants to make life hard for us and that He withholds good things from us. They assume that He must use lack and difficulties in order to force us to cling to Him. We've been falsely taught that only judgment and trials will keep us humble and repentant before Him. We forget that it is only "the

---

[119] Galatians 3:13; Romans 8:32; John 10:10.

[120] Psalm 27:3.

[121] 2 Timothy 1:7. The word translated as "power" is the Greek word for "force," or specifically, "supernatural power" (Greek 1411 from *Strong's Exhaustive Concordance.*

[122] Andrew Wommack, *Spirit, Soul, and Body.*

goodness of God that leads us to repentance."[123] Our hearts are softened toward Him when we see how generous and loving He truly is.

We still don't fully grasp the riches that are ours in Christ or the abundant life we were meant to live. If Jesus truly took all our sins and sicknesses, as well as the curses, we can now live in the blessings. By faith in Him, we can live in peace and confidence as lights in this dark, troubled world. We are called to bear witness of His goodness and provision.

We look at our situations and perhaps see many problems, and then we interpret scripture in light of what we see. Circumstances are never a reliable indicator of truth; only God's Word is. We can't build doctrinal premises around situations that contradict what Jesus has done for us. All the writings of the New Testament clear tell us what is now ours in Christ.[124]

In taking our sins, Jesus gave us righteousness and acceptance with God. When He took upon himself the curse, he availed for us the blessings. The apostle Paul said that we were once under the curse because of Adam.[125] Because Jesus carried our sins in his own body, the curse had to come upon Him instead of us, even though He Himself had never sinned. He suffered the consequences of our sins. He conquered them and rose from the dead, and now in Him, we can receive the blessings instead of the curses.

If Jesus suffered to give us these things, then certainly it is God's will for us to have them! If you are sick or in lack, fear, or worry, if you're experiencing trouble and devastation in your life, you don't have to stay there. You are God's son or daughter, and He has something better for you.

In his letter to the Ephesians, Paul prayed that their understanding would be enlightened so that they could know, or fully comprehend, the meaning of this "hope" and "the riches of the glory of his inheritance" that were in them—and are now in us.[126] He wanted the Ephesians to grasp and experience the "exceeding greatness of His power toward us who believe."

Paul went on to expound on the reality of this power that is in us, telling them that this is the very "same power that raised Christ from the dead and set him at the right hand of God, far above all

---

[123]   Romans 2:4.

[124]   Colossians 1:13; Ephesians 4:7–20; Galatians 3:9.

[125]   Galatians 3:13.

[126]   Ephesians 1:18–23.

power, might, and dominion, and every name that is named." These "names" include depression, fear, and poverty, diseases and conditions like diabetes, arthritis, cancer, and celiac disease, to mention just a few. God bestowed this power on the church, for His Spirit abode within them (as it now abides within us).

Further in the same letter, Paul spoke of our being "strengthened by His Spirit in the inner man" so that we can know and comprehend this great provision bestowed upon us by His love. Whenever we spend time in fellowship with God, we can be strengthened and solidly grounded in the reality of what is ours in Christ.

Paul closed by saying, "Now unto Him that is able to do exceedingly abundantly above all that you could ask or think [or even imagine], according to the power ["supernatural power" in the Greek] that works [is active] in us."[127] Yes, we have this power within us through our connection with God, but it wasn't meant to simply lie dormant in our spirit.

On a similar note, Paul's letter to the Colossians spoke of his concern that they be comforted in the "full assurance of understanding of this mystery" regarding what is ours in Christ. If we have Him, we have everything that we need for every situation!

"For in Him dwells all the fullness of the Godhead bodily. And you are complete in Him, which is the head over all principality and power."[128] In the Greek, the word translated as "complete" speaks of being "full to the extent of making replete": that is, to cram (into a net), level up a hollow, or furnish and satisfy.

When we pray and express our needs or desires to Him, we can truly pray with thanksgiving, as Paul instructed us to do,[129] because we're not waiting for Him to decide whether or not to answer. He has already given us, through Christ, everything we need. In fact, He doesn't send us anything apart from Himself, for He has come to dwell in our hearts, and through this relationship we have access to all things that we need.

In this walk, we have to know what is ours in Christ, what is possible for us, and what is expected of us.

Think, for a moment, of some of the seemingly radical things that Jesus said and did. He healed the sick, raised the dead, calmed the waves and

---

[127] Ephesians 3:20.

[128] Colossians 2:9–10.

[129] Philippians 4:6.

wind, multiplied the loaves, and did many other things. You might say, "Of course, He was the Son of God." The average Christian has no problem recognizing the things Jesus Himself did during His earthly ministry, but many choke on the idea that we too can do some of these things. Jesus often alluded to the fact that they—through faith—were also called to do great things. He said, "All things are possible to him that believes."

We easily acknowledge the teachings of Jesus on justice, repentance, generosity, and so on. Many Christians have memorized the Beatitudes and even the Ten Commandments. We aspire to live this way and rightly so. Incredibly, however, we skip over passages where Jesus made clear reference to the fact that we could—and in fact, were expected to—do the same and expect the same results. When, for example, He spoke of faith that could move mountains,[130] He didn't say, "Pray, and I will move the mountain" or "Ask God if He is willing to move the mountain for you." In essence, He said, "Speak to the mountain [the challenging situation in your life] and exercise the faith and authority that is now yours,"[131] and the mountain will move.

Our mountains may not move immediately, but if we continue to stand on and speak God's Word in our hearts and to the situation until our faith is strong, things will change for the good.

In many scriptural accounts, we read about Jesus instructing his disciples and expecting them to do some amazing things. Even more amazing is the fact that the qualification for doing these things is to be one of "them that believe." This, I assume, means us too.

There was a time when the disciples were in a boat and a storm rose.[132] In one account of this situation, Jesus was sleeping, and the disciples were in panic mode. They knew that in such a storm their boat might not hold up, and they would probably capsize. They woke Jesus, and He calmed the storm. But oddly, he admonished them afterward, asking them, "Where is your faith?" What else could this have meant except "Why aren't you using it?" In some versions, the phrase "in Me" is added to the question "where is your faith?," but I have found that this wasn't included in the original text. The point is that we too have a responsibility to use the faith and resources He has given us.

---

[130]   Mark 11:22–24.

[131]   Luke 10:19.

[132]   Mark 4:36–41.

Going back a little further to just before the situation in the boat, we see that Jesus had been speaking to a crowd of over ten thousand people.[133] It was getting late, and they hadn't eaten. Jesus said to his disciples, "Give them something to eat." They talked about how far from any town they were and how much it would cost to feed so many—as if Jesus didn't know. They didn't yet grasp the principles of faith that He had been teaching them. Could it be that He was giving them an opportunity to exercise their faith? I believe this was the case.

Looking back at an even earlier situation, we read about a boy who needed to be healed from epilepsy. The disciples, observing the severity of the case, couldn't heal him. Again, Jesus gave the impression that He didn't want them to ask Him to do it. He said, in essence, "O faithless and perverse generation, how long shall I put up with this?" When they asked him why they couldn't cast out the spirits, Jesus told them plainly that it was because of their unbelief.[134] In all these cases, he expected them to do the job.

Interestingly, just prior to this, Jesus had given them authority and sent them out to preach the good news, cast out devils, and heal the sick.[135] Certainly He expected them to continue doing so.

So has He also called and equipped us, for He said, "These signs shall follow them that believe."

I'm not talking about faith in ourselves or in our ability to believe. God wants us to step out in the faith He has invested in us. Having our foundation resting upon what Jesus has done for us, we can take authority and speak to the mountains in our lives.

When I was a child, there were many subjects in school that I enjoyed and did well in, but math was not one of them. When it came to solving math problems, it seemed like an insurmountable barrier looming up before me. Many times I'd whine to my mother that it was just too hard and I couldn't do it. Out of her concern, I suppose, she did me a disfavor; I discovered that I could get her to do it for me.

From the start God has draws us to come to Himself and His provision through Jesus has accessed for us all that we need for this life and beyond. He is always with us and willing to work on our behalf.

---

133   Luke 9:12–17.

134   Matthew 17:17.

135   Mark 6:7–8, 13.

But we have a free will, and we must choose to believe and take hold of what He has given us. It is our responsibility to take hold of what is ours in Him. Day by day, it is our choice whether or not we walk in life and victory.

After Jesus's resurrection, Peter and John approached the temple and encountered a crippled man who was begging there.[136] We don't see them praying and asking God if He would be willing to heal this man. No! They knew it was His will. Instead, we see Peter saying to him, "I don't have silver or gold to offer you, but what I do have I give to you. In the name of Jesus Christ of Nazareth, rise up and walk." And that he did, leaping with joy and praising God.

If we are believers, we too have this potential within us, and we cannot let it lie dormant. It must be expressed in our lives and actions. Don't be afraid to speak a word of faith over a sick person. It's not your ability or name that is at stake; you're standing in the authority of God's Word. If you speak in faith, He'll back you up. You're representing the finished work of Jesus. We can simply say, "In the name of Jesus, receive your healing," for we are representing the name that is above all names.

You can speak God's Word of blessing, healing, peace, and victory over your own life and situation. Instead of worrying, fretting, and doubting, we can take charge over the Devil's work of deceiving, lying, and stealing. We don't have to put up with that. Jesus conquered him and has given us authority. He has equipped us in every way.

Paul, in speaking of the promises of God, confidently assured us that all of them, in Him, are yes[137] and are certain for us. Every good intention that God has ever had in mind for mankind—and has recorded in scripture—is ours, in and because of Christ. To emphasize his point, Paul assured believers that his message was sure, not in doubt or undecided. He went on to say that the promises God predetermined for us are not a case of "maybe or maybe not," "sometimes yes and sometimes no." Rather, in Christ these things are an unalterable fact.

The most amazing thing about God's promises is the fact that they are ours—as Paul put it, "unto the glory of God and that by us."

You might ask, "How in the world can all God's promises—our health, welfare, prosperity, success, and everything else the promises

---

136 Acts 3:1–10.

137 2 Corinthians 1:17–20.

include—be to the glory of God?" The fact is that He is honored and exalted when we, by faith, take these promises into our lives. We are His representatives in this world, and our lives and testimonies reflect His goodness.

In her book *Blessed Beyond Measure*, Gloria Copeland tells us that God wants to bless us. She says that "all through scripture we see God wanting to give His people such abundance and victory, that it would get the attention of the heathen." She quotes Deuteronomy 28:10, where it says that in this way "all the people of the earth shall see that you are called by the name of the Lord." In Jeremiah 33:9, God says that the fact that His people will be blessed will give praise and honor to His name before the nations.

Then, by way of contrast, she shares how Isaiah points out the fact that God's name was blasphemed before the nations when His people were beat down in captivity.[138]

In Psalm 35:27, David wrote, "Let the Lord be magnified, who takes pleasure in the prosperity of His servants." In the Hebrew, the word translated as "prosperity" is the word *shalom*, which means "welfare and health; to be safe, well, and happy; prosperity and peace."

God equips us to be His representatives, His ambassadors. What president, prime minster, or king would send out representatives who are sick or ill equipped? If these ambassadors have needs, resources are immediately sent to them.

We have a job to do: we are representatives of His kingdom.

You might say, "Well, I don't have that kind of faith!" or "We're not all called to be Pauls or Peters or even John G. Lakeses"—or any other great minister you may have heard of. The fact is that we don't have to be like such people. We are not all called to be great ministers, but we are all equipped for greatness. God chooses the weak and those who feel unqualified for the job, using them in impossible situations. He is God, and He is confident in the power of His Word invested in us.[139]

It's time for us to walk in this new life He's given us, that His good name may be magnified in the earth.

---

[138]   Gloria Copeland, *Blessed Beyond Measure* (Tulsa, Okla.: Harrison House Publishing).

[139]   Isaiah 55:10–11.

CHAPTER 23

Congruency: Living in God's Reality

"Vision without execution is nothing."
—Kevin O'Leary

There is no denying it; God is good, and His Word is true. His loving character is trustworthy and dependable. His wisdom and principles are right and beneficial. Jesus's provision is real and sufficient. We find all these things to be so as we appropriate and apply them in our lives.

Many Christians have recognized the reality of this powerful potential that is ours in Christ, and yet few of us fully apprehend it in personal experience. It's not because it is too hard or beyond our reach. No! God didn't intend this walk with Him to be difficult or complicated.

Remember how easy faith was when you first began this journey. You may have been struggling with personal issues or wrestling with doubts and fears, but the moment your heart turned to Him and made that connection, peace was yours, and confident faith set you on the path to victory. We may have thought that was the end of it, but it was just the beginning. God expects us to continue in this way through His enabling grace. He wants us to live in sweet fellowship with Him and to enjoy this new, abundant life He has given us.

We all long for peace, and we crave stability and victory in our particular situations. We want our lives to count and to have a positive effect on the world around us, because if our faith doesn't work in real life, what do we have?

All of God's Word and principles demand application; otherwise it's only information.

Perhaps we assume that application only involves "going" out there and "doing" something for God. We may think that "bearing fruit" means doing evangelistic work to bring forth new Christians. We assume that our faith is all about obedience and good works, and we wear ourselves out trying to bear fruit. Or perhaps we are just too busy trying to survive in this world, and bearing such fruit has eluded us.

We all know that these things are part of a fruitful life, but before fruit can grow, the ground has to be prepared and nourished.

Paul spoke of the qualities that we possess in Christ, and he typifies them as "fruit" of the Spirit, speaking of attitudes, attributes, and character. Bearing fruit involves more than just good works; it has to be the overflow of what's happening inside a person. We bear fruit when our lives and attitudes reflect the new, righteous nature that is now within us. A tree or plant doesn't have to strive or perform to bring forth natural fruit. It simply flows out of the plant's internal capacity.

When we fully believe and accept what Jesus has wrought for us, our whole perspective of life will change. The premise behind every decision we make will be based on Jesus's finished work and who we are in Him. We will see every challenge we encounter in light of the power and provision that is ours in Him. This realization sets us on the path to living in God's reality.

But how do we consistently and effectively appropriate God's Word—that is, the new covenant realities—into our lives?

The application of God's Word must first be internal, in our hearts and thoughts, before it can extend into our lives.

God's reality is based on what Jesus has done for us. His perspective hasn't changed from the Old Testament to the New, for this has always been His heart and desire for us. Life, peace, health, restoration, and abundance have always been His intention for us in this world.

In this fallen world, we encounter a very different reality that sometimes contradicts God's. Our everyday experience does not always find us in peace, health, prosperity, or victory. Our faith, sense of purpose and empowerment, and all the things Jesus has purchased for us seem to wane with our changing circumstances.

We ourselves often hold to an opposing view of reality. Our perspective of life, of others, of the world around us—and in particular, of ourselves—is not always in line with God's perspective or evaluation. Nevertheless, this is what we accept as our reality, and we live our lives out of this carnal mind-set.

Our view is not always accurate. It is often influenced by faulty and distorted perceptions of reality. Some of our opinions and biases are subtle and subconscious and have, in fact, simply been taken on and carried with us from childhood experiences. Our perceptions of our experiences become our reality.

As a child, I believed that I was of little worth, inferior and inadequate. Because this became my premise, I began to interpret every word and attitude of those around me as confirmation of this faulty view. Although as a young adult I recognized intellectually that this wasn't true, the feelings in my heart still kept me bound to that old perspective—until one day God's love enabled me to see myself in a different light.

When I first met my stepfather, he held strong, negative views of German people. He used to say, "Never trust a German." He believed that they were all arrogant and heartless. As the years passed, he became close friends with a couple who, it turned out, originated from Germany. Little by little, his views mellowed. When I asked him about it, he told me that his father had fought in WWII and had seen the atrocities of Hitler's regime first hand. Consequently, Ronny had taken on his father's attitudes, even though he himself had never fought in the war and never had any negative experiences with any German people.

When we're in default mode and not trying to be, feel, or act better, we relate to life and act in accordance with our perceptions. Consequently, our trust in God, His Word, and His reality can be distorted, and our faith can be impaired. Then we cannot clearly recognize the goodness of God, much less live in this reality.

Often we see what is possible for us through the promises and provisions in scripture, and even though our hearts witness to the truth, we can't accept it, much less apply it. So we continue to live in a way that is inconsistent with what Jesus has done for us.

In my own experience, after a dramatic initial encounter with the Lord and two years of walking in this newfound reality, I found that a sense of His love was always present, faith was easy, and even healing was always within reach. I joined a church, experienced the joy of fellowship with other believers, and gained some scriptural foundations. But little by little, I began to notice personal inconsistencies. I understood how I should be living as a Christian. I saw it in the Bible in the fruits of the Spirit, the Beatitudes, and so on. It was often the subject of sermons.

I couldn't deny the changes in my attitudes and perceptions that had taken place in my heart at the beginning of my walk. Yet within a few years, I became aware of the return of old patterns of behavior, and certain situations inevitably produced particular reactions in me. Many times I'd find myself in conflict or at odds with other people. I'd pray about it and ask God to change me—and then wallow in self-condemnation, but that didn't help anything.

Then, in a similar situation, I'd find myself reacting in the same old ways. I tried to act loving and kind, but that was all it was: an act, a performance. Nothing on the inside had changed. I was told that God was dealing with my wicked heart and that He wanted to purge away the sins of my soul. But difficult situations and people didn't produce any real change in my heart. I needed something deeper, for I was seeing through the eyes of childhood experiences and faulty perceptions instead of God's perspective.

Seeing these inconsistencies in my own life, I realized that the solution involved more than reading the scriptures and attempting to change or act differently. Something had to happen internally.

The inconsistencies we experience have their root in something deeper than external sins (in the sense of evil deeds). Rather, they are rooted in the heart where our faulty perceptions lodge.

First, Jesus's provision has to be appropriated and applied in our hearts, and then God's Word has to be internalized. As I mentioned earlier, everything God does in this new covenant time, He does from our hearts. He speaks to us in our hearts, and we commune with Him in the secret places of our hearts. It's here that our deepest beliefs, our sense of self, and all our underlying perspectives reside.

Jesus's victory is complete, but in case you haven't noticed, it doesn't happen automatically in our lives. Just because we don't see it, or it doesn't seem to be working consistently in our experience, doesn't mean it's not true or not for us in this present time.

We've been given a free will, and God will never force His will—or even His provision—on us. Through Jesus's suffering and victory, His work is finished, and now in a real sense, "the ball is in our court." Now we must choose to accept what Jesus has done for us. By faith, we can appropriate these good things into our lives so they can be a present reality.

The whole Christian life is a process of growing in view of this. When we first come to Christ, we encounter a whole new paradigm, and maturing in Christ involves making this our premise.

It's a walk of faith, and we can choose our perspective in every situation.

Scripture encourages us to focus on and attend to God's Word and not allow it to depart from our eyes but to keep it in the midst of our hearts."[140] Joshua was instructed to meditate on God's Word: the laws, principles, and perspectives.[141] Even Moses, in reading the laws to Israel, spoke of God's words as being in people's hearts, though they didn't yet have the Holy Spirit living in them.[142] Paul told Timothy to meditate on the words and principles he had taught him.[143] David said to the Lord, "Your Word have I hid in my heart."[144] Many others scriptures speak of meditating on the truth. This is how we establish our hearts and our thoughts in God's Word.

It's not enough to simply read the Bible. We have to internalize the principles, personalize the promises, and of course, understand it in view of Jesus.

Meditation is not some strange and weird practice where you sit cross-legged in a cave on a mountain, nor is it just something practiced in yoga. In biblical meditation, you are simply setting your focus on God and His Word. It's a means by which we can establish our hearts in new covenant truth.

In the same way that we easily rehearse and rehash negative things—like a disagreement with someone or a problem we're facing— we can also meditate on God's realities. We mull over negative things quite naturally without much effort. Sometimes we worry and imagine the worst outcome in a situation. We meditate this way until even our emotions are stirred. This is how we write something on our hearts and it becomes a deep-rooted perspective—like a prejudice

---

[140] Proverbs 4:20–24.

[141] Joshua 1:8.

[142] Deuteronomy 6:6–9.

[143] 1 Timothy 4:15.

[144] Psalm 119:11; Psalm 15:1; Proverbs 4:20–21.

or conviction—until eventually our lives reflect a particular attitude without even trying. How much better and more beneficial it would be if we were to meditate this intensely on the truth of what is ours in Christ.

Jesus said, "Take heed what you hear."[145] We must be careful of what we spend our time listening to or thinking about. In Mark 4:1–20, Jesus was teaching through the parable of a sower scattering seed. He explained various scenarios in which seeds were unable to take root and thrive. In the end, he explained that the seed, which represented the Word of God, was sown in the "good ground" of the heart by those who heard the Word and received it. In the Greek, the word *hear* speaks of taking heed or giving attention to something, and the word *receive* means to accept and delight in something. It reminds me of Proverbs 4:20–21 where it says, "Attend to my words."

In Mark 4:24, Jesus said, "Take heed what you hear." Then He went on to explain: "With what measure you mete out it shall be measured to you: and unto you that hear [give attention to it] shall more be given."[146] In other words, the amount of attention we pay to the Word, reflecting on and thinking deeply about it, will cause it to increase in our lives.

I believe He meant that the more attention or consideration we give to His Word, the more we will get out of it.

Meditation is a tool we can use to strengthen our faith in new covenant realities.

You can make meditation a regular part of your daily devotion or prayer time. It's a good way to start your day with a new covenant perspective.

Many times I meditate on identity scriptures such as: "I am accepted in Christ" Ephesians. 1:6; and "I am a new person in Christ." I Co. 5"17; or "I am righteous in Him." and so on. In the Greek and Hebrew the word meditation means: to revolve in your mind, imagine, and to muse pensively to murmur, and to ponder.

Kenneth Copeland says, "We must make God's word or final authority." (not feelings, circumstances, or the problem we're facing) If our habitual thoughts deny what Jesus has done for us, it's time to change our thinking and renew our perspective. Proverbs 16:23-24 tells us that "The heart of the wise teaches his mouth and adds learning to his

---

[145] Mark 4:24.

[146] King James Version.

lips. Pleasant words are like a honey comb sweet to the soul and health to the bones." There is power in the words we speak. In Proverbs 1:6, we are told that the words of the wicked lie in wait for blood, but the mouth of the upright shall deliver him." The Devil tempts us and torments us with words, but our words have the power to deliver us.

We apply and appropriate God's Word in our own lives by first establishing our hearts in faith. Faith is a vehicle by which we can see the unseen realm of God's reality.

It might seem obvious, but I believe it's worth saying: confessing God's Word is not just something we do in our personal quiet time with the Lord; it is something we must do in everyday life. One day I began to notice what I was thinking on a regular basis. In various situations, particular words that were contrary to new covenant truth habitually flowed out of my mouth.

It has taken some time, but now, instead of saying things like "I'm so worried about that" or "I don't know if I can do this," I say things like "I can do anything through Christ who strengthens and enables me." If I lie in bed, tempted to worry, I say, "Thank you, Lord, that You are with me as You promised" and "I can always anticipate His help." In order to maintain a true (new covenant) perspective, we must ask ourselves, in every situation, "What does God say about this, in view of Jesus and His finished work?"

It's a process of renewing our minds in light of who we are, what we have, and what is possible for us in Christ. It takes an effort to begin with, but if we keep at it, our hearts will soon be established in the new covenant.

Don't allow religious thinking to cloud your vision.. God is not mysterious or unknowable (as some would have us believe), and He does desire to bless and equip us (Jesus spoke of His good will and suffered to avail us access to His goodness.

What we believe is so important. We must have a clear and accurate understanding of the whole gospel truth. When we are settled in new covenant realities, we have a solid foundation for our faith.

Jesus has availed for us an abundant and superior life, and we can choose to live in this reality today. This, after all, is what the Christian life is really about.

ABOUT THE AUTHOR

Margaret Belanger is an avid writer; she has written a book of poetry, as well as several personal journals. She has also written letters to the editor of several newspapers (on various political issues). As well, she has written and illustrated 2 children's book (as yet unpublished).

Margaret is also a creative artist (specializing in acrylic paintings). She is a retired Art and Bible teacher of 20+ years. She presently teaches ESL part time.

Her writing reflects her teacher's heart as she articulately communicates "new covenant realities" of which she is passionate. Margaret Belanger is very happily married and lives with her husband on a semi-rural acreage just outside of the picturesque valley of Smithers, British Columbia, Canada.